HAUNTED
WINCHESTER

MATTHEW FELDWICK

TEMPUS

First published 2006

Tempus Publishing Limited
The Mill, Brimscombe Port,
Stroud, Gloucestershire, GL5 2QG
www.tempus-publishing.com

British Library Cataloguing in Publication Data.
A catalogue record for this book is available from the British Library.

ISBN 0 7524 3846 8

Typesetting and origination by Tempus Publishing Limited.
Printed in Great Britain.

CONTENTS

A panorama over the ancient and much haunted city of Winchester from the commanding position of St Giles Hill.

INTRODUCTION

The supernatural has always played an important part in the background of the city of Winchester. There has forever been, lurking around every corner and propping up every bar, a story or a legend which purports to the paranormal in some way or other.

It is unsurprising, given the city's wealth of history, that ghosts are said to haunt almost every inch within the old city walls. A fair number of hitherto unreported hauntings that have come to light during the course of writing this book are included within these pages.

Along with the ghosts and spectres are included, for good measure, some of the legends that are retold from time to time. These range from the famous St Swithun with the rain and the eggs to the less well known Peter de la Roches and his brush with King Arthur.

The stories told here are collected from a variety of sources, not all of them reliable, since many a yarn has been recounted to me over several pints of beer or in return for a bottle of wine and there are a couple of tales reported here which I know to be fraudulent. However, I feel that it would be wrong not to include them with the others as they represent part of the art of storytelling and, after all, the old saying does suggest that there cannot be any smoke without fire.

I would like to express my thanks to all those who have aided and abetted me in the pursuit of stories for this book; to Vicky for her constant support and encouragement; and to the good citizens and shopkeepers of Winchester who have invariably been more than willing to share their knowledge. Many has been the time I have presented myself unannounced to the shocked shop assistant demanding tales of the supernatural or visits to their cellar and, to their credit, I have been welcomed.

Therefore, what I present to you here is an account of my favourite hauntings and legends that have been recorded in and around the wonderful city of Winchester!

Matthew Feldwick
March 2006

SELECT BIBLIOGRAPHY AND FURTHER READING

Chilcott-Monk, J.P., *Ghosts of South Hampshire and Beyond*, G.F. Wilson and Co. Ltd, 1980

Fox, I., *The Haunted Places of Hampshire*, Countryside Books, 1997

L'Estrange, A., *Royal Winchester*, Spencer Blackett, 1882

Long, R., *Haunted Inns of Hampshire*, Power Publications, 1999

Telford-Varley, Revd, *Winchester*, Adam and Charles Black, 1914

Underwood, P., *Ghosts of Hampshire and the Isle of Wight*, Saint Michaels Abbey Press, 1983

Underwood, P., *The A-Z of British Ghosts*, Chancellor Press, 1971

Underwood, P., *Hauntings*, Dent, 1977

one

From the Buttercross to Hyde Abbey and Return

It is perhaps easiest, especially for those not acquainted with the intricacies of the city streets, for us to take our haunted tour on an area by area basis. Consequently this book is first split up into two short walks through Winchester, with a further chapter on those hauntings which fail to fit into either of these paths. The final chapter will take a brief look at some supernatural activities which occur within a few miles of the city.

History and ghosts always go hand in hand and in such a place as this, whose human history stretches from before written evidence, a retrospective look at times and people who have gone before us is unavoidable.

The Buttercross

We shall start our perambulation to Hyde at the Buttercross, for the simple reason that it marks the spiritual centre of the city. At one time all distances were measured from here and it still remains a principal meeting place. The cross was constructed during the reign of Henry VI and remained in its original form until the inimitable Gilbert Scott 'restored' it in 1865. He replaced three of the four main statues in the niches and had eight further saints added in the alcoves above. Of all the great men of the city he chose the following to be depicted as the principal statues: William of Wykeham, King Alfred the Great, and Florence de Lunn. While the former two would be well known to those who have even a basic knowledge of Winchester's history, the latter is something of an enigma. De Lunn was reputed to be the first mayor of the city, and in a prime example of Victorian one-upmanship became highly venerated; a sort of 'we can trace our mayor's lineage back further than you!' To my knowledge there exist three statues of him on public display in the city, a memorial stone in the Guildhall and a set of buildings

A lone woman sits on the Buttercross; does she not realise the curse to which she is subject?

The mythical, although well represented, figure of Florence de Lunn.

in Jewry Street named after him – more is the pity that there is scant evidence for his actual existence!

During the eighteenth century the city corporation, ever keen to make a profit, sold the cross to a Mr Dummer, who intended that it should serve as an ornament in his formal gardens. However, when his workmen arrived the city revolted and he was effectively thrown out of the West Gate. The people of Winchester are good at rioting and have demonstrated this natural skill many times over the centuries.

The Buttercross is also the site of our first legend of Winchester, and I hope that if you are reading this book out-of-doors that you are standing in the High Street rather than sitting on the monument in question. This unsubstantiated story has been told time and again, of a curse which was put on the Buttercross in the middle ages by a witch who was held here before being burnt at the stake. Effectual from the moment an individual's posterior contacts with the stone, the curse compels the unwary sitter to return time and again to the city. Numerous examples are cited: people who sit, move away, and yet are forced to revisit or even move back. Such is the pull of the Buttercross! A lesson for all unwary travellers is to check with local folklore before sitting anywhere!

The Buttercross is supposed to play host to its own ghost. Rarely seen, except for the occasional glimpse when the old Guildhall bell is toiling the 8.00 p.m. curfew, a shadow is reputed to approach at speed from the west, under the Pentice and behind the Buttercross, where it disappears towards the Cathedral. I have only managed to track down two people who have witnessed the apparition and their descriptions, although agreeing with the above portrayal, differ in their view of the spectral shape. One reported that it was the figure of a man in long dark cloak while the other thought that it was more like a large dog or child. I have attempted many times, as the curfew rings out loud and clear, to see the shape for myself, but alas to no avail.

God Begot House – ASK Pizzeria

Passing up the High Street, towards the West Gate, we have only to go a few yards when we are confronted with the imposing half-timbered building of God Begot House. While the front has been tidied and made to integrate, as far as it is possible, with the rest of the of the High Street, Royal Oak Passage alongside gives a most splendid vista on this most ancient building. Here the timbers remain in much the same way as they have been for the past 500 years. Granted a charter by Queen Emma and being of ecclesiastical character, one of the privileges ascribed to it as a building was one of sanctuary, allowing it to act as a place of refuge for those trying to escape the law. A number of skirmishes took place here between the church and the civil law upholders, with people being physically dragged from the building. It also served as a law court and judgements often took place here. During the reformation it was seized from the monks of St Swithun by Henry VIII but was passed almost immediately back to the prior; the reasons for this remaining unclear to this day.

One possible explanation for this change of heart by the monarch could be the curse said to apply to God Begot. Wading through the Middle Age descriptions of the curse two things become clear: firstly whosoever takes the manor by force is condemned to an eternity in the devil's own cauldron and, secondly, the butchers of hell would be at liberty to carve the transgressor's flesh forever.

It is therefore a little sad to report that the substantial part of God Begot is now an outlet for a franchised pizza restaurant.

A fair number of human bones were found here about 100 years ago when the building was being converted from a bookshop to a hotel. It was thought at the time that these bones may have come from a Saxon cemetery on the site and it could have been this discovery which prompted the spectral manifestations associated with the building.

It was the drawing room of the hotel which was supposed to be haunted. Nothing physical was ever reported to have appeared but strange rapping would be heard at intervals around the room. So disturbed was the owner that he had the whole building exorcised. Dogs could not be persuaded to enter that particular room; they preferred to sit outside and howl. After a knock residents would call for the person to come in, thinking that it was a maid, or would even open one of the doors to let the unseen entity in. With successive remodelling of the building over the past century all trace of this room has now gone and the knocking with it. That, however, is not the end of strange goings on at God Begot – recently the sound of crashing has been heard in the cellar. Perhaps it is the displaced ghost of the old drawing room or a new ghostly spirit?

God Begot House, where the faint echoes of a colourful past can still be heard.

Royal Oak Passage

Although this pub, The Royal Oak, has yet to reach the status of a trendy wine bar it has been heavily altered in image and in internal layout during the past few years. Notwithstanding this, it still boasts to be the oldest bar (as opposed to inn) in England and certainly parts of the building date back to Saxon times. There is a tradition that one of the many tunnels that radiated from Winchester Castle surfaced here before continuing to William the Conqueror's palace, although no trace remains today.

Back in the passage outside, there have been several reports over the years of chanting monks and whisperings heard hereabouts. During and just after the Second World War, tales have been told of shadowy, transparent figures sighted. These spectres, wearing cassocks rather than the habits of monks and walking as though in prayer, were witnessed by an old Winchester resident as he stepped out of the Royal Oak at closing time one evening in 1947. From his account he almost fell on three figures as he passed through the pub door and was able to watch them slowly walking towards the High Street. Although sure of three ecclesiastical persons, he felt that there could have been more, unseen, forming a procession with which he was caught up. Lasting only the short length of the passage he felt himself drawn with them, as though floating rather than walking, and as they neared the start of the building fronts so they became more transparent, fading away to nothing by the time they reached the High Street proper: he was left hanging on to a lamp-post vowing not to touch strong beer again. He said that he was so frightened by what he saw that he ran home with his eyes almost continually shut, arriving in such a state that his wife thought him blind drunk!

The passage originally ended at the small church of St Peter in Macellis, long demolished, although the outline has been picked out in the paving where it stood, which could be the originating place for the witnessed procession.

The whisperings heard in this vicinity, when at their best, seem to start at the end of the passage and move down to the High Street as though a couple or group of persons are in conversation. At other times it is only a snatch of dialogue which is heard. Never are the words discernable or the discussion long in length. Mr John Flint, a long time resident of the city claimed to have heard voices as he took the passage as a short cut home from work in the 1970s and early 80s. He thought for years that it was a conversation taking place between shop workers in God Begot house until a change in use caused the building to be empty for a while. He is convinced that he heard the whisperings of Royal Oak passage!

In recent years these echoes now seem to reverberate infrequently. No reports have surfaced for a while now, although by all accounts, ones chance of hearing something is heightened when exiting the Royal Oak after consuming a goodly number of pints!

Retracing our steps to the High Street we continue in our journey ever upward. Near the junction of Jewry Street stood the George Hotel.

Royal Oak Passage, where whisperings and ethereal forms are said to occur.

The George Hotel

The stable block that once stood to the rear of this establishment, which was far older than the rest of the hotel, was scene to a very nasty incident in 1643. At the outset of the Civil War Sir William Waller supported the Parliamentarians and became chief commander of their forces in southern England, gaining many famous victories over the Royalists including Farnham, Chichester and Winchester Castle. Loyalties were divided in the city but the predominance of support was towards the King. Since Waller's army were unpaid every opportunity was taken by them to loot the town and to generally disgrace themselves.

Prized only slightly less than gold was a horse and Master Say, Royalist and son of a cathedral prebendary, owning several fine animals, directed his servant to take them away and hide them from the marauders. Unfortunately for him, his servant sympathised with Cromwell and betrayed his master. Dragged before Waller, he was questioned over his conduct and when his answers were deemed unsatisfactory, was transferred into the custody of the Provost Marshal; the intention being to obtain a confession.

Say was taken to the stable of the George and a bridle placed around his neck. Still he refused to talk. His torturers then proceeded to haul him up and down, slowly strangling him by degrees and very nearly killing him. Those who had come to witness the event were appalled by the conduct and persuaded the perpetrators of the spectacle to cease this horrendous torture.

However, the mark of this horrific event was left upon the building, even after 300 years, and remained until the stables' demolition after the war. Stories are still told among the older generation of how noises would be heard in the vicinity of the old stable. Strange sounds such as the 'rasping, guttural cough of a dying man' and the 'scrape and heavy thud of wood on cobbles' would be perceived by patrons and staff alike. However, since Barclays Bank has stood on the site all has been quiet.

Waterstones

I suspect this can apply to most if not all cellars and basements around the country: someone at sometime has heard a noise emanating from beneath them. Logical explanations are always readily available; badly or hastily stacked items are always falling over, heating pipes and floor joists expand and contract, and, of course there are always rats. However, the supernatural option of 'it must be haunted' is most often employed and there are at least five haunted cellars in the High Street itself! I do not wish to record them all here since one story is very similar to the rest. Waterstones is a typical example though.

According to one former member of staff, she had heard 'skriffings' and crashes from the basement of Waterstones on a regular basis when the shop was quiet and had not liked it at all, nor could she be persuaded go down into it! With the kind consent of the current store manager I was allowed to visit the said cellar and take the photograph reproduced here. Although it was very dusty and practically abandoned I failed even to catch an 'orb'!

The dusty and grimy basement of Waterstones.

The old Hampshire Chronicle Offices

On the opposite side of the High Street stands the rather forlorn and empty building which up until 2004 housed the offices and at one time the presses of the *Hampshire Chronicle* newspaper for almost 200 years.

Obviously there was great sadness from the *Chronicle* staff at having to move from a site with which they had had links with for so long. However, it was not the logistics of the move which concerned them, rather the question of whether their resident ghost would be accompanying them. Editor Alan Clever expressed the fears of the staff in an article published in the *Hampshire Chronicle* on 9 June 2004:

> When I broke the news to them I thought I'd thought in advance of every question they might ask but when they wanted to know if the ghost was coming as well I was truly lost for words! And now I just don't know what to do. Do I leave our grey lady a map? Do we leave a seat for her on the removal van – just how do you 'move' a ghost? I think that after nearly 200 years of wandering the corridors of the *Hampshire Chronicle* she might appreciate a change of scenery.

There had been many reports of supernatural activity over the years at the offices and these were frequently reported in the newspaper, usually as a filler article. At least two different apparitions have been reported in recent years, firstly that of a woman accompanied by a clanking noise, and secondly that of a man outside the file office. The latter phantom was encountered by sub-editor Lesley Park neatly around Halloween time in 2001. According to her account published the following week in the *Chronicle* the following is said to have happened while she getting ready to leave for home at about 6.30 p.m. I am grateful to a former member of the *Chronicle* staff for a paraphrased version and newspaper clipping recording the event.

She was making her way to what were the advertising offices when she noticed what appeared to be a figure of a man standing outside the file room studiously examining a pile of newspapers. As she watched, the form began to turn and walk through what later transpired to be a locked door into the file room itself. At that point she decided to give chase to what she now realised was a ghost and not an intruder. Swiftly moving to the spot where she had last seen the figure, she could find no trace of the visitor.

When a group of paranormal investigators, during the making of a television documentary, spent the night in the offices they reported that some interesting revelations had come to their team during the stay in the building. *The Phantom or Fraud Project* came equipped with all the latest in electronic wizardry; infra-red cameras, EMF detectors, which record fluctuations in electro magnetic fields, and a whole host of clairvoyants and investigators. While they did not witness any materialisations, they did come up on some parts of the buildings past. The spirit of a man was sensed in the editorial office, perhaps the same one Lesley Park saw, and another medium picked up on that part of the offices had been a pub until the turn of the twentieth century. The strangest revelation was from one psychic who claimed to see chickens in the staff training room.

The 'clanking woman', as she was described to me, has been seen and heard in part of the premises previously occupied by a large tenement known as La Peryne, demolished in 1897 to make way for the present building. Here there was a small printing press and it is to this that the sound has been attributed.

The former well-haunted offices of the Hampshire Chronicle.

I contacted the *Hampshire Chronicle* in January 2006 to ascertain whether they had been successful in persuading their ghost(s) to make the journey to their new offices in Staple Gardens but learned from a member of staff that to date there has sadly been no sighting of anything unusual.

Turning right into Jewry Street passing Barclay's bank we continue on our ghost hunt through the city centre towards the parish of Hyde.

Winchester Library

Winchester Library, the former Corn Exchange, has been reputed to be haunted for a good number of years. It was built in 1838 and served as the Corn Exchange. It cost at that time the exorbitant figure of £4,000, reflecting the importance of the building and the trade at that time to the city. By the turn of the century it had ceased to be a popular place for trade and was put to a variety of different uses including as a dance hall and a roller skating rink. From 1915 it was used initially as a theatre before being converted to a cinema. In this guise the building also hosted a restaurant and a tea shop. In 1936 the City Council, who had bought the building some twenty years previously, moved the public library here. Hence, with all the changes which have taken place during its history, it is not surprising that some echoes of the past have been left behind.

Within the building footsteps have been heard and there have been reports of singing from the basement. It was the caretaker who first heard the footsteps one morning in the early 1990s before staff arrived for the day. According to all accounts they appear to be walking around the mezzanine balcony which runs around the edge of what was the great hall. He gave chase, thinking that there was an intruder, and after a thorough search of the entire building, checking the still securely locked and fastened doors and windows, he was forced to admit that the sound had not been generated by an earthly being!

The basement of the library is interesting architecturally in itself. The stone vaulting which supports the weight of the building and the damp unease produced by being underground is enough to conjure up any number of spectres. Spooks rattling chains and vampire bats are what one would expect down there, but not the sound of operatic singing! According to the librarian, who had worked there for many years, the voice was faint but still distinct and that there was no musical accompaniment. As she moved around the basement to try and ascertain where the sound came from so the singing faded to nothing. She walked over to the trapdoor from the street in case the sound had originated from there but all was quiet. However, returning to her original position the singing could still be heard. Puzzled by the whole experience she related the tale to a colleague and suggested a return to the basement. Unfortunately when they returned to the spot where the singing had been heard they were only greeted with silence.

On a recent visit to the library I was told, in no uncertain terms, that there had not been any reported activity in the library recently, with the inference that these stories had been made up. The basement has been effectively sealed for several years and the library is about to undergo a massive transformation internally. It will be closing from February 2006 for a significant period of time to allow the building of the Winchester Cultural Centre. Much of the preparation work has been undertaken already, including the rediscovery of the Second World War air-raid shelters, complete with period graffiti, and ancient artefacts of Roman and Medieval Winchester. One wonders what ghosts will be raised by this action and whether those which have haunted here will be laid to rest.

The former Corn Exchange, Winchester Library, with its singing and footsteps.

The Theatre Royal

The Theatre Royal was built during 1913 by brothers, John and James Simpkins and enjoyed a modicum of success during the First World War, but by 1922 was mainly showing films and in the capacity of a cinema operated until 1974 when it closed. From 1978 it has largely been run by enthusiasts and since its recent rebuilding and restoration it has gone from strength to strength with always an interesting production on the bill.

The Simpkins brothers were deeply passionate about the building of their theatre and agreed to discuss each detail before it was finalised so that each could have the same input into the scheme. It was almost inevitable that disagreement would creep in and, as so often is the case, it was over the most trifling of issues. Brother James, without the agreement of John, ordered a decorative boss to be arranged over the proscenium arch which contained the initials JS. John thought that this should read J&JS and, after many hours of bitter arguing, persuaded James to change it.

However, with the intervention of the First World War and the subsequent death of John the amendment to the initials did not take place. Even to this day this oversight grieves the wraith of John who periodically leaves what was his office before walking around the circle, stopping half way to examine the proscenium to see if the requested change had been executed. With apparent sadness the ghost then drifts away…

Another event that is reputed to have taken place at the theatre happened during the First World War. With conscription claiming all the young men for the trenches of Europe the staff

The exterior of the Theatre Royal.

of the theatre became quite depleted, and James was starting to amass quite a sizable photograph album: it was his tradition that if one member left the company for the army he would gather all the staff together for a farewell photograph.

One of those who left for the trenches was the spotlight operator, who was dating one of the principal actresses. One evening during a musical review she fainted and had to be carried off stage, unable to continue with the rest of the programme.

James came up to her after the show had ended and she had composed herself to ask what had been the matter. She divulged that she had seen her sweetheart in the prompt corner of the stage where he used to work the spots.

The telegram to his mother giving notification of her son's death arrived the following day.

As a postscript, others have seen this apparition and more recently, that of his love, the actress, around the theatre and have been able to identify them from the poignant farewell photographs taken by James.

According to one former employee, a number of years ago during the 1970s restoration, footsteps were heard making their way up the stairs to the circle by the manageress of the bar. Thinking that it was intruders or burglars they rushed into the theatre only to find all doors securely locked and the place apparently empty. The area where this took place has changed radically since then and no reports of any spectral footsteps have been heard for many years.

Since the reopening of the theatre in 2001 two further unusual events were witnessed by a current employee. The first strange thing occurred very shortly after the theatre had started trading once more. It was before opening time and the staff were busy in preparation for the performance.

Theatre Royal interior, showing the circle which is reputed to be haunted by the wandering ghost of a former owner.

To the ears of one female member of staff came the distinctive sound of the theatre's piano being played by an expert hand. Since the only person on the team capable of playing so well was on holiday, she went into the auditorium to investigate. As she opened the first door into the theatre so the music faded to a stop. She walked in and found that not only was the place deserted but the piano was pushed up against the side of the stage with its dust cover still firmly fastened. No explanation for what she had heard has ever been forthcoming.

The other odd happening seems to take place in the new lift. When the theatre was rebuilt the shop alongside was also incorporated to give additional space and to allow the improvements required by modern health and safety regulations. Such an improvement was the installation of a contemporary, stainless steel lift and it is within this item of modern machinery that strange lights have been seen. From all reports a little speck is seen glowing against an internal panel on a very regular basis. Initially thought to be caused by something shining through a crack in the casing, this light has no preference for where it appears. Sometimes it can be seen when the lift reaches the top of the building, while every so often it is observed throughout the duration of travel. A paranormal investigating team spent the night here not so long ago and captured a great number of 'orbs' on film. They too reported that there were 'balls of energy' to be found in the lift.

To continue along this tour, head over City Road and proceed along Hyde Street for our next set of ghostly encounters…

The Hyde Tavern

Even if not the oldest inn in Winchester, of which it boasts, the Hyde Tavern can trace its roots back to the times when monks still lived at Hyde Abbey and the city was a strong walled fortress. Hyde Abby was for many centuries the resting place for the bones of the only English king to have the name 'Great' added to their title. King Alfred's bones rested here until the eighteenth century when the ruined remains of the abbey were torn down and used in road construction. However, local legend has it that the bones of Alfred were saved and re-interred in nearby St Bartholomew's church. Delving back into legend we find that it was here that the raiding Danes sent a giant to put fear into the inhabitants and to win the city through single combat against the English champion. Brains overcame brawn that day and the illustrious Dane-slayer, Guy of Warwick, was declared a hero. The area by the river has been known as Danemark since that time.

The tavern is everything one could possibly want from an ancient building: there is not one level surface in the entire building, the timbers are properly jointed without the need for modern nails or screws, and it has an interesting history. Several times during the nineteenth century it had its licence revoked due to the unacceptable conduct of its patrons. The last time it was shut for this reason was in 1860 when the landlord was prosecuted for allowing bare-knuckle fighting to take place. The half sunken inn today boasts fine beers and a fine haunting.

The story goes that several hundred years ago on one foul winter night the then landlord of the pub refused a poor woman food and lodging. Her frozen body was found the following morning on the doorstep and since then strange things have happened for which there is no apparent explanation.

It was not unusual for those staying at the inn to find themselves disturbed as they tried to sleep. The night would start with no evident problems and most people would say that the rooms were comfortable, if not a little basic. The trouble would start a few hours after the lodger had gone to bed. They would discover, usually to their chilly horror, that their bedclothes had been pulled off their bed. All logical explanations can be dispelled with this haunting: it could be that the sleeper had kicked the blankets off in a dream, but not that they had tied them up and dumped them in the middle of the floor! It is not beyond the realms of possibility that some living body, with motive or motives unknown, could creep into the room while the guest slept and perpetrate the act; although with the door remaining securely locked and bolted and the high windows too small even for a child to crawl though this seems unlikely.

Added to that, if the visitor was unlucky enough to be a light sleeper then they might perceive something invisible, perhaps accompanied by a cold, clammy atmosphere, slowly dragging their blankets from their beds!

No matter how well the beds were made or how tightly the guests were tucked in, inevitably the bed they slept in would be stripped by morning.

The bar area is also affected by the presence of person who delights in placing a frozen hand on the arm or shoulder of an unsuspecting drinker. This chill presence has been felt many times in living memory especially during the winter months when the fire is burning warmly in the grate and the tavern is barricaded from the unruly elements outside. Could the bedclothes removing incident and the above be the manifestation of the woman who froze to death for want of a landlord's charity?

The Hyde Tavern.

Hyde Abbey

As mentioned earlier, Hyde Abbey was the resting place of King Alfred the Great and the site of Winchester's second most important place of medieval pilgrimage. Hyde Abbey originated from what was known in the city centre as the New Minster. This church was completed in 903 and became the resting place for several holy relics and the bones of Alfred, his wife Ealhwith, and latterly his son, Edward the Elder. Being right next door to the Cathedral space was at a premium and Henry I, wishing that the new Norman Cathedral should have all the sacred space in the heart of the city, ordered that the New Minster to be moved to Hyde. From then on the church became known as Hyde Abbey. With all due pomp and ceremony the bodies of the king and his family along with the holy relics were processed to their new home in 1110 and for several centuries the abbey enjoyed a fair amount of success, becoming quite prosperous.

When Henry VIII dissolved the abbey he did so with such zeal that barely a trace remains, save for the gate house and fragmented bridges over the abbey stream (reputed to be reconstructed by the Victorians anyway). However, it appears that not all the monks left when the Abbey was sacked.

There is a passage which runs behind the church of St Bartholomew, a building itself almost a 1,000 years old in places, and it is here that the phantom is supposed to walk. A local resident claims to have seen the apparition a number of times over the years. The dark, hooded figure, presumably that of a monk, is often seen progressing along the passageway towards the tower end of the church, always disappearing at the point at which the path curves before reaching the main entrance to the church. The first time the monk was spotted by this now quite elderly gentleman, he admitted to being very scared at what he saw: 'It didn't go away, it kept walking away from me, head bowed and wearing a brown habit'. The classic ghost monk – a textbook example.

Since that time he reports that there was seldom a week that went by in the early 1990s when he didn't see the apparition. Sightings since then have become fewer and fewer; the last report he was able to give was of October 2005. This personal spectre does not appear to have been witnessed by anyone else but there are plenty of other accounts of monks and nuns in the vicinity. The path which leads one along the stream eventually to Kings Worthy church is known as Nun's Walk. Originally called Monk's Walk, local tradition states that the name gradually got changed due to the spiritual presence of a nun-like figure seen from time to time. What a nun was doing near a monastery, something which was generally forbidden, is open to conjecture.

We return at this point back to the city centre through the passageways among new housing to North Walls and from there along Parchment Street.

Parchment Street

While the 1973 book by Patricia McKillip, *The House on Parchment Street*, which tells of a young girl visiting her cousin in England and helping troubled ghosts in the cellar, sits well in this street it remains just a story. The real ghost of Parchment Street appears to be that of a spectral mist which moves from a corner near the old chapel along the road towards the High Street. A Winchester resident, who lived for a number of years in this road, told me that she witnessed

No misty apparitions today. Parchment Street where such a form has been encountered.

Opposite above: *The only remaining part of Hyde Abbey, which surprisingly does not appear to be haunted!*

Opposite below: *The passageway behind St Bartholomew's Hyde, where a monk still walks.*

'something rather strange and peculiar' one winter's evening before the Second World War as she was getting ready to go out for a night at the pictures in Eastleigh. What she reputedly saw lasted at most a minute but was probably no more than few seconds, yet it has remained indelibly etched in her memory ever since.

It was just after 6.00 p.m. when her friend called for her and slipping on her coat they made their way towards the bus station via the High Street. They had gone only a few yards when her friend noticed a black shape two houses away from them. This form then began to drift out towards the middle of the road turning as it did so into a light wispy mist. Scared as the young ladies were they stopped and watched the vapour swirl and move away, all the while getting smaller and less distinct before disappearing altogether.

At this point their nerve failed them and quickly turning they retraced their steps before going to the bus station by a different route. It would be many months before either of them had enough courage to walk down that road after dark again!

And here ends the first haunted walk through the city's streets. Continue along Parchment Street, cross St George's Street and rejoin the High Street outside Boots. Turn right and arrive back at the Buttercross.

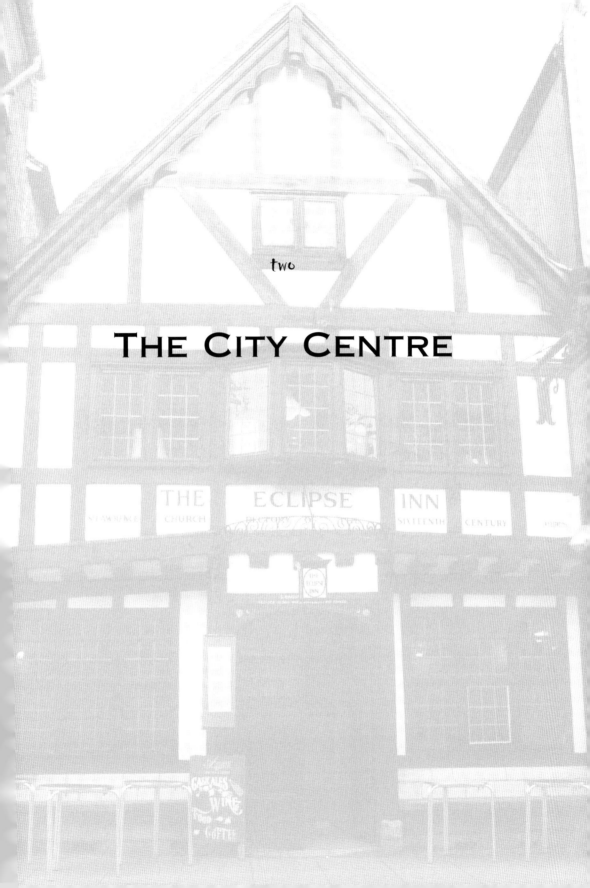

two

THE CITY CENTRE

The second of the two tours outlined in this book takes us on a gentle stroll through the ancient heart of the city, past the Eclipse Inn, the Cathedral and around the lower east end of the ancient capital within the limits of the antediluvian (a nice Roman word, fitting well within the context of this sentence) boundary and the remains of the city wall.

As ever we start off from the Buttercross, mentioned at length in the previous chapter, and head off towards the south and the Cathedral; passing through the passageway by St Lawrence's church we emerge into the square and find the chilling tale of Dame Alicia Lisle…

The Eclipse Inn

The Eclipse Inn stands in the probably the most misnamed street in Winchester. Although there is nothing unusual in calling an area 'the Square' it is usually called because the area in question bears resemblance to a quadrangle. The Square in Winchester is more of an 'L' shape which withers away into part of the infamous one-way system that characterises the city for the car driver.

The Eclipse is situated near the bottom left junction of the 'L' and is a charming sixteenth-century building. Initially constructed as the rectory for St Lawrence's church it was heavily rebuilt in the 1920s when during routine maintenance the original façade accidentally disintegrated. However, it was painstakingly copied so that none of the enchanting features would be lost.

This is probably the most noted and well-documented haunted location in Winchester. The pub is most celebrated for one of its visitors who stayed, alive at least, under the roof for one night only.

Winchester Cathedral from Southgate Street. (W.J. Hart)

Dame Alicia Lisle was the widow of John Lisle and lived most of her life at Moyles Court, an Elizabethan house near Ellingham in the New Forest. John Lisle was an eminent judge in the seventeenth century and he was one of those who sentenced Charles I to death. Although this was his most high profile of judgements, it was one that he made several years before, concerning the execution of a John Penruddock, which would be the source of trouble for his wife.

John Lisle was murdered in his bed at Moyles Court in 1676 and with his death the safety of the family name began to falter. Dame Alicia escaped much of the persecution that surrounded such families after the restoration of the monarchy in 1660, but Colonel Penruddock, the vengeful son of John Penruddock, brought the seventy-one-year-old lady to Winchester in 1685 to stand trial.

She was tried under the infamous Judge Jeffries as one of a series of cases which would be later known as the 'Bloody Assizes.' The charge brought before her related to the unsuccessful Monmouth rebellion which had started on 11 June 1685 as an attempt by the Protestant James, Duke of Monmouth against the new Catholic King, James II. She was accused of harbouring two dissenters after the battle of Sedgemoor at her house and such a crime warranted public execution. Despite her pleas of innocence and inconclusive evidence, Judge Jefferies convinced the court that she was indeed guilty. He sentenced her to be dragged through the city of Winchester before being subject to the most hideous of deaths – burning at the stake.

The elders of the city and friends of the family were horrified at this judgement and convinced Jefferies to put a stay of execution for five days. The Cathedral and clergy along with the city then petitioned the King to change the penalty. James II, wanting to show compassion and leniency, responded by altering her punishment to one of decapitation.

The famous Eclipse Inn with the active ghost of Dame Alicia Lisle.

Consequently, Dame Alicia was taken from her prison in Winchester Castle and held overnight at the Eclipse prior to her execution. A scaffold had been built outside the building and on 2 September 1685 she walked out of an upstairs window to keep her appointment with death. After a short execution speech in which she condemned Jefferies at length while praising the clemency of James II, the axe fell swiftly and her body was removed for burial in the thirteenth-century church at Ellingham.

With such unfair circumstances surrounding her death it is not surprising that her ghost is reputed to walk the corridors and haunt the upstairs rooms of this pub. The 'Grey Lady' is a frequent visitor and there are numerous people including former landlords and regulars who will testify to strange phenomena being seen and a sense of unease and brooding being felt. I spoke to one former landlord who knew nothing of the story of Dame Alicia until he took up the lease. On the first day he was there he entered into one of the upstairs rooms and had such a feeling of sadness and fear that he only ever reluctantly re-entered the room after then. If you should find yourself at the bottom of the stairs do not be too surprised if you feel somebody invisible brush past you or an odd chill pass through your body.

Dame Alicia is an active ghost, since her wraith has also been reported haunting Moyles Court and at her son's house, Dibden Manor, where she is said to appear in classic decapitated style with her head tucked safely under her arm. There have also been reports of a ghostly coach and horses – all headless – carrying her back from Winchester to Moyles Court, although this has not been witnessed in the city itself.

There is another ghost story reported that may be connected to this public execution, or perhaps to another – there were a fair number taking place in the square during the Middle Ages!

Around 1947 a young and impressionable journalist was making his first solo reports on criminal trials which were taking place at Winchester Crown Court. Having misjudged the length the trial he was reporting on he decided to spend a pleasant afternoon exploring the many and varied delights of the city. Exhausted from touring the city's streets and the Cathedral he stopped off for afternoon tea in the Cadena Restaurant which had commanding views along the length of the High Street. Being seated in the window he was able to observe the patterns and habits of shoppers as they went about the process of shopping. Suddenly he was surprised to notice that a large group of people in old, what is now described as period, costume making their way from one side of the High Street, approximately where W.H. Smith stands, towards and through Boots. While still puzzling on what he had seen a short time later some of the group reappeared, but this time further up the High Street by the passageway which leads to St Lawrence. Somehow he could see that they all looked distressed and that some were even in tears.

Summoning the waitress he enquired about a possibility of a pageant being held nearby and received the surly reply that there was no such thing happening on that day. He promptly paid and went on an investigation of his own to ascertain the nature of the procession he had seen. Arriving at Boots he discovered that there was a back door to the building through with the group could have passed and on passing through himself he found that he was in the square near to the Eclipse Inn and the city museum.

The curator of the museum was very helpful. There had been no pageant that day but where Boots stands was once a passageway and remains a public thoroughfare. Since the square was the setting for a number of public executions, the curator speculated that the young journalist had witnessed the ghost of a procession on its way to an execution and then its depressed return after prayers has been said for the departed soul at St Lawrence.

As far as I am aware this spectacle has not been repeated either before or since. A local historian confirms the plausibility of the actions of the citizens since it is documented that prayers were often said prior to and after public executions at St Lawrence's church.

To continue on our tour cross the road outside of the city museum, well worth a visit if you have the time and the possible site for a haunting – a member of staff once saw a man in a very thick coat walking around an exhibit in the middle of summer. Thinking it odd a few minutes later she went to see where this person had gone only was unable to trace the mysterious figure. She admits that it could have just been a tourist that had decided to wear an anorak on the hottest day of the year and that the person had slipped out of the museum when she wasn't looking, but she doubts it!

The Hambledon

It is here that we have another example of the famous haunted cellars of Winchester. This example, although the story is not that remarkable, is worthy of inclusion solely on the setting alone! The great vaulted arches and heavy atmosphere of this basement tell of a far earlier building than the Georgian edifice which now occupies this spot.

The Hambledon is best described as an eclectic lifestyle shop. It sells only that which its owner, Victoria Suffield, would be willing have in her own home or would wear. It does contain some very fine items from all over the world, although since I am a mere man I am unable fully to comprehend or to give the merchandise justice through prose! Nevertheless, well worth a visit!

The close proximity of the building to the site of William the Conqueror's palace raises the fanciful possibility that the stone arches holding up the shop may have been an integral part of this earlier building or a mint or of the many of buildings that would have sprung up, acolyte-like, around the royal abode. Whatever their original intention there have certainly been some strange noises reported from these cellars, especially about a hundred years ago.

The haunting which supposedly takes place here is in the form of poltergeist activity. During some modifications, so I have been reliably informed, in the 1880s small articles where thrown about, glasses would be knocked off tables and smashed on the floor some distance from where they were placed, and objects had a habit of disappearing and rematerialising in unlikely places. Gradually as the decade wore on so these events grew less and less until the only activity was the sound of items being moved about or perhaps the sound of a breaking glass. Now, 120 years later, the supernatural activity has all but stopped.

Therefore while being a historically haunted location it should not be discounted for future manifestation: plans are in place, about to be executed, which will see the shop undertake some alterations to their basement, to open it up as an additional sales space. I only hope they do not use the area to display glassware!

The wonderful cellar of the Hambledon.

Winchester Cathedral West End.

Winchester Cathedral

I apologise in advance for the next fifteen hundred words; they are rather heavy on the history and light on the hauntings but I feel justified in placing them here since it sets the background for some of the strange things which have been experienced in this part of the city…

As with many old church sites worship has been conducted on this sacred, hallowed ground since pagan times. Below the current crypt there is a well similar to the type found around the country noted as holy wells and transformed by the early church to hold a Christian reverence. The Romans built their temples here too; and there is evidence to suggest that these were to Concorde and Apollo. To accommodate these, the Romans diverted the river and built for it a new course roughly where it is today forming the eastern boundary to the old city. With the early spread of Christianity these temples were swept away and a church built. The church of St Amphibalus under the monks of the order of St Mark the Evangelist was said to be the largest building in the city at the time, although we have no real evidence even for its existence. After a great persecution the church was said to have been rebuilt by Constans, the son of Emperor Constantine, who then became the priest to the city. The church then entered a long period of peace, shattered by the marauding Cerdic when he landed at Southampton in AD 495. Despite the great battles fought by a leader of the Romano-Britons, perhaps the closest figure we can show in history to the great King Arthur, the country was converted to the old Saxon religion. The monks were slain and an image of the god Woden set up inside the church. Cynric, son of Cerdic, had some very nasty dreams and started to rebuild the church in Winchester. Under the guidance of Cenwalh the first Cathedral appeared around AD 648 and, with the arrival of the bones of St Birinus, miracles started to take place.

The legendary St Swithun lived, worked and died here, bringing wealth to the Cathedral and to the city, and we shall hear some more of him throughout this book, although admittedly mainly of his post-mortem achievements. The legend of the rain on St Swithun's day comes from this period when, only nine years after the death of the popular saint, monks tried to exhume the body. With the spade cutting the first sod there came an almighty clap of thunder and the rain which followed lasted for forty days.

Æthelwold undertook the rebuilding of what was starting to be known as the Old Minster and it is during this time that we read for the first time of a miracle.

It appears that one of the stonemason monks was working at a height one day and had a slight fall. Construction was going to plan, if not a little slowly, and a haste was being made to have part of the building finished for the feast of Swithun. The monks engaged on the task were working for as long as there was light and unsurprisingly it happened that one misjudged a distance and seemingly fell to his death. However, no sooner had the monk had touched the ground than, on making the sign of the cross, he was lifted back up to the place were he had been working. According to the onlookers who witnessed this extraordinary sight the monk simply took up his trowel and recommenced his work where he had left off!

Wolston, the great chronicler of his day, waxed lyrical about this sacred place with its multitude of chapels and altars, with the large labyrinth of a crypt and the adornment of gold and silver on every part of the edifice. With the removal of the bones of St Swithun into the Cathedral, this time without thunder and rain, the number of miracles increased dramatically, as did the coffers of the church. It was reported at that time that is was almost impossible to get near the Cathedral due to large numbers of sick and diseased all lining up to be cured by the saint.

Skipping forward through the years we come to the tenth century and to Queen Emma of Normandy, who was accused of impropriety with Bishop Alwyn, tried and condemned to prove her innocence by walking over red-hot plough shares. Spending the proceeding days and nights in prayer before the shrine of Swithun she received assurance from the saint that no harm would come to her. The following morning she was brought before a great crowd assembled in the Cathedral and nine plough shares were fetched out and heated red hot. Four were set for the innocence of Emma and a further five to prove the incorruptibility of Alwyn, who had conveniently been dead for several years.

With the cry of 'Oh God, who didst save Susannah from the malice of the wicked elders, save me' she commenced her walk, eyes cast heavenwards in prayer. She sensed nothing and after a number of steps stopped and enquired to one of the bishops on when they would be reaching the plough shares. He replays that she is standing on the last one. After one final step Emma's feet are examined and are shown not to have even the slightest mark. Those who brought the accusations were seriously admonished and banished from the country with a sound beating, while Emma received back all her lands including God Begot (see earlier story).

With the arrival of William the Conqueror, the city of Winchester started to change and move more towards the city we know of today. The Cathedral was rebuilt in its entirety for one further time by William and finished by William Rufus and it is from this foundation that we date the current building. Bishop Walkelin laid out the plans in 1079 and by 1093 the building was sufficiently complete to be consecrated. Timber for the roof was a major concern of the bishop. However, being a persuasive man, he talked King William into allowing the felling of as many trees in the forest at Hempage near Avington as could be undertaken in four days. The King capitulated to the request and the bishop stripped all bar one tree from the forest. The King was not pleased and there remained for a fair while a feeling of enmity between the two parties. As an aside, the tree which remained was a Gospel Oak under which it was reputed that St Augustine had preached when he first brought Christianity to these shores. The iron fettered remains of this tree are still in place.

This Norman monstrosity was even longer than the building we see today and had an impressive tower topped by a tall spire. The story of the downfall, literally, of this tower is worthy of note. On 2 August 1100 there was a mishap in the New Forest where King William II, better known as William Rufus, was accidentally shot by an arrow which, according to some accounts, landed in an act of irony in his eye. Whether the debatable unfortunate incident was actually an accident or whether it was preconceived murder we shall never know. He was not a popular monarch and by all contemporary accounts it was fortunate his reign was ended before he could undertake any further damage to the country. With William Tirel, who shot the arrow, and the other members of the hunting party fleeing the scene, it was left to a local carter to bring the body back to Winchester. Custom has it that he was once buried in the large black stone sarcophagus which one trips over when processing through the Cathedral choir, directly under the tower.

During the above paragraph it was mentioned that Rufus was not popular. The truth of it was that the Church detested the monarch for his milking of the wealth of the Church and his practice of raiding the monasteries whenever he had a shortfall. Hence, when the tower collapsed in 1107 it was widely held that either God was not pleased with the final resting place of the King or that the evil influence of the departed monarch still pervaded after death – the holy Cathedral, unable to contain or suppress the still-emanating wickedness, dealt with the problem by falling down!

The choir of the Cathedral is worth an examination, if only to pay homage to the relics now stored in the mortuary chests balanced high on the stone tracery. These chests contain the bones of some of the Saxon kings and bishops, including some of the heroes from the text above: Cenwalh, Emma, Alwyn. The bones of the Danish King Canute and others are also here. Now neatly stored and preserved they met with some excitement during the Civil War between the Roundhead Puritans and the Cavaliers. The Roundheads had taken the Cathedral by storm and promptly set about destroying anything which was contrary to their religious views. The statues in the altar screen were removed and broken up and the self-promoting effigy of Charles I was decapitated. This was later hidden on the Isle of Wight and restored to the Cathedral in 1660. All the stained glass was destroyed at this time and being unable to reach the high glass they utilised the bones from the chests as missiles! Thankfully these were collected by the good people of the city and hidden for the duration of the Commonwealth.

William of Wykeham.

Continuing with our historical synopsis, Bishop Eddington rebuilt the west front of the building to the style which we see today. The great William of Wykeham spent a considerable amount of time and a fair amount of money in the reconstruction of the Cathedral from the drab Norman building with its heavy architecture to the light lofty structure which was to epitomise the style of church design until the twentieth century. On his death he left 2,500 marks to complete the work. Wykeham was responsible for the foundation of many great institutions both within Winchester and elsewhere, including Winchester College, and it would be very fitting to say that his ghost haunts the Cathedral, but unfortunately it does not.

Additions and deductions have taken place to the fabric of the Cathedral over the centuries with much of the finery being lost or plundered by thieves, be they ecclesiastical, imperial, or material. The literal downfall of the Cathedral almost came about a century ago when the river, diverted by the Romans, proved once and for all that a river can not be deviated from its course. The original foundations to the building were great trunks of wood encased in clay to stop them rotting. The diverted river over the centuries had, however, returned to a sufficient degree to wash this clay away, thus allowing damp and rot to cause the decay of these timbers. With the imminent collapse of the east end and south side of the building serious consideration was given to the complete rebuilding of the structure. William Walker, a diver from Portsmouth, was called in and working over a number of years in the black water under the Cathedral replaced the rotten wood with bags of cement; one of the earliest large-scale underpinning accomplishments.

Enough of the history lesson and a much needed return to the myths, legends and ghosts! With all the upheavals and changes over the millennia one would expect the Cathedral to be bursting with ghosts. Where is the unhappy wraith of St Swithun? One would expect him to make the occasional appearance. Perhaps the removal of his skull to Canterbury and his arm to Peterborough has quelled this potential spectre! However, not all of the former worshipers appear to have passed so quietly on…

One quiet summer's day in 1957 the Taylor family from Wolverhampton, spending a few days on holiday in Winchester, visited the Cathedral. Nothing apparently strange happened to them within the building nor did they notice anything untoward during the rest of their stay in the city. It was only when they returned home and had the photographs developed that they noticed something strange had happened in the Cathedral. Mr Taylor had taken two pictures of the carved stone screen behind the high altar roughly from the position of William Rufus' tomb; one of them was perfectly normal, but the other, taken only seconds later, appeared to show thirteen shadowy figures in medieval clerical dress. There were no other people about nor could the forms be reflections of the statuary which adorn the altar screen. The photograph attracted a great deal of attention as various members of Winchester clergy tried to disprove the validity of the image – even the *Daily Telegraph* carried the story!

One of the ghosts of the Cathedral that only ever makes a rare appearance is that of a grey lady. She is said to haunt the south transept and was seen by one verger during the early years of the last century. I'm unsure quite how it happened, but he was so terrified of what he saw that he managed to break both his legs shortly after the incident. No sightings have been reported for many years, although a sound technician working in the south aisle during October 2005 reported to me a couple of days later that he thought he had felt something repeatedly brush past his arm, for which he could offer no logical explanation.

The greatest plethora of paranormal activity around the Cathedral can be found within the close, not surprisingly often concerning the spectral figures of monks which once occupied this site. Open as a thoroughfare to the public between 7.00 a.m. and 10.00 p.m. one must be careful not to get locked in.

The gateway to No. 11, The Close is reputed to be haunted by the hooded figure of a limping monk. There are, as ever, a number of conflicting stories about this compelling story, yet it still remains one of the most interesting hauntings of the city. According to a former member of the Cathedral staff, who does not wish to be identified, the ghost is supposed to appear by the wall to the right of the gate before making its way slowly and painfully in a direct line to the south door. The spectre passes straight through a flying buttress (which is an early twentieth-century addition) before dematerialising at the door itself.

During the 1920s and '30s this apparition would be seen on a very regular basis particularly by the wife of one of the canons and it has been reported since on a very infrequent basis. During the late 1930s the wall from which the form was said to emanate was rebuilt and during the reconstruction of the foundations three bodies were found all dated to pre-Dissolution. One of these was buried facing towards the east, then signifying a man in holy orders and, to add further interest to the discovery of corpses on a haunted site, it was revealed that there was evidence for extreme arthritis on the left knee of the skeleton; the same leg on which the apparition is said to limp.

Winchester Cathedral's modern flying buttresses; a monk limps though the middle of one!

Cherney Court with St Swithun's gate. The thundering of horses hooves have been often reported here.

The strangely named Dome Alley which leads off the close has been the scene for numerous strange happenings during the nineteenth and twentieth centuries. Perhaps the most reports are that of the sound of horse's hooves ringing out as though passing along cobbles at speed. The last mention of these sounds I received was in November 2004 from a friend who was passing through the close at about nine in the evening. From the information I was able to extract from the garbled answerphone message and subsequent conversations it transpired that a sound 'like that of several horses thundering beside me in the street as though in a race' had been heard that evening starting near St Swithun's gate and galloping with increased volume along the close and down Dome Alley. The sound stopped abruptly and the city continued as though nothing had taken place.

Number 7 Dome Alley was, at one time, a haunted house of the classic type. It had been the home to Izaac Walton, the famous author of the *Compleat Angler* and the room in which he used to write is the place where a finely dressed woman in a hooped skirt has been frequently seen. At the same time, in the drawing room, there sits a woman with at least two children at her feet listening intently while she silently reads from a book. Within the nursery a moving figure, never seen, opens and closes the door at one end of the room, passes through and exits through the door on the opposite wall, again opening and closing it with care. Half an hour later the otherwise undetectable spirit returns, passing through in the same way as it came.

Back in the Cathedral close again the sound of chanting and the sight of ghostly monks has been witnessed by tourists and residents alike. A particularly favourite place for the chanting to be heard is under the Cathedral library in the south transept. It is here where the Norman architecture still survives largely unaltered and apparently so does Gregorian chanting! This spot is always breezy; even on the stillest day there is usually a strong wind funnelled through the passageway at this point. Could it be that the accounts refer to the noise of the wind whistling around the ancient stones rather than a supernatural cause? If this is true, why do others report seeing a group of monks heading along the path by the east end while hearing the sound of ethereal singing?

One other ghost story that is worthy of inclusion in this compilation of tales from around the Cathedral happened in the 1920s and was relayed to me by the gentleman who had experienced it. In classic style, it was a dark and damp evening, of the type only Winchester can produce – a wet drizzle that drenches through to the bone. The boy music scholar was running back into the dark and locked Cathedral to collect some music from the organ loft and return it to the master. Bounding up the stairs to the organ console and then down again he had no thought for ghosts or spectres. Reaching the bottom of the steps a sound made him stop; the curtains that separated one of the chapels from the transept was moving! To his horror the curtains parted and in the darkness the dim outline of a nun in full habit emerged into view. Unsurprisingly, he ran! The nun followed, and by this time was starting to talk. Terrified, the boy ran at full speed out of the Cathedral and out into the close where he was met by a friend. Unable to speak, trembling with fear, all he could do was point as the nun came out of the door. The apparition spoke, 'I'm afraid I must have dropped off while praying in there; could one of you boys direct me to where the rest of my group might be?' It was a real nun who had been on a sightseeing trip to the Cathedral!

We continue our tour by passing under the south transept, following the route of the chanting monks, and walk past the east end and the Lady Chapel along the passageway known as the Slype. Note how the building leans out at this point; a lasting reminder of the poor foundations.

Worthy of observation is a little bricked up archway, on your left, leading from the footpath as a private entrance to the house which lies behind the Cathedral wall. Legend states that Charles II, who wanted to rebuild Winchester into a grander version of Versailles, was responsible for the doorway being knocked through the wall. On his many visits to the city he would stay at Wolvesey Palace, while his wife, Catherine of Braganza, when she occasionally accompanied him, was lodged just outside the city walls. The famous orange seller and mistress of Charles, Nell Gwyn, would often accompany him though and this posed a bit of a problem. The Bishop, understandably and rightly, did not wish for illicit relations to take place on church property and especially not in Wolvesey Palace. Charles conceived a plan; he had the house behind the wall bought for Nell and undertook the door in the wall to be cut. This meant that all he had to do was to sneak out of the palace, through the door at the end of the passage (still in use today), and in through his private entrance to her residence. The bishop just tolerated this and on Charles' death the doorway was bricked up never to be spoken of again!

Turn left at the end of the passage but beware of a sharp shove by an icy hand as you do so!

Slype Passage where a mischievous ghost prods and pushes older women.

Slype Passage

I was talking to an old colleague of mine about nothing in particular in this very spot when she suddenly dropped into the conversation that she didn't like the gateway or the passage between it and Colebrook Street. It transpired that every time she passed along it she would stumble over something unseen or receive a push in the small of her back. Once she went cold all over within a couple of yards of entering the Slype and had to turn back, shivering and shaking with fear. She had spoken to some other female friends and they too had felt similar, although not as vivid, feelings and agreed with her that they sometimes felt something pushing them.

Intrigued, I laid in wait by the passageway for a few hours one sunny Tuesday afternoon and questioned a number of people on the subject. Of those interviewed, no male reported anything strange ever having happening to them there, nor did any young female. Of the 'slightly older' ladies questioned two described something unusual happening in the area. One had felt feelings of unease and coldness while the other, in her fifties, described a sharp shoving from one side several times over the last year.

As far as I can ascertain there are no records of anything untoward happening hereabouts and certainly no apparitions have been sighted, but I think that this is one possible haunting which may well become clear with further research.

Cross over Colebrook Street and head along Abbey Passage.

Abbey Passage, Abbey Gardens and Nunnaminster

Until the excavation of the 1970s little was known of the structure, nor did any excavated trace remain, of Nunnaminster, latterly known as St Mary's Abbey. This nunnery stood on the site now occupied by the Mayor of Winchester's house and the formal gardens and public park conceal the remains of most of the abbey. It was founded by the wife of Alfred in 899 and survived until the dissolution of the monasteries under Henry VIII.

This was another site for miracles in medieval Winchester for it was here that the shrine of St Edburga was located, until its removal a couple of hundred years later. Edburga was a nun of royal descent. She was the daughter of Edward the Elder and the story goes that on her third birthday she was offered the choice between a small chalice and paten or gold and jewels for a present. She chose the former and her life long vocation was sealed. She was sent to Nunnaminster and became noted for her holiness and piety. On her death she was buried in a simple grave under a simple stone within the minster. Nuns reported that they were unable to close a window which overlooked her burial place and soon reports of miracles started to occur. The holy nun's body was exhumed and a costly shrine decorated with topaz and precious metals was built before the high altar. Miracles continued to happen and the shrine became quite important and profitable. However, in about 974, Bishop Æthelwold brought about the movement of most of the mortal remains of the saint to the newly re-founded abbey at Pershore where she was venerated in her own large chapel for centuries. It appears at first sight that the removal of the saint from Nunnaminster was short-sighted on their part since she was the main source of their revenue. However, it transpired they were very well paid for the relic; which goes to show that the abandonment of heritage for short term capital gain is nothing new!

The almost empty shrine remained a place of pilgrimage for the next few hundred years but without the abundance of miracles there once were, so the shrine and the abbey fell from popularity.

All that remains of the abbey today are the excavated remains from the Guildhall extension and the ghost which is supposed to haunt the passage. Of the former, on the left, between the passage and the Guildhall, are a collection of stone sarcophagi and the outline of the ancient footings of the building, which have been picked out in coloured stone. The perfect place for scaring children and not a few adults!

The ghost, unsurprisingly, is that of a nun, head bowed walking either through Abbey Gardens or along Abbey Passage. She is one of the commonly sighted apparitions which frequently walk around the city. No fewer than four separate reports were received by me during 2005. She is usually sighted around the middle of June, which leads to speculation as to whether this is the wraith of Edburga, since her feast day is the fifteenth of that month. Conceivably it could also be the spectre of another nun, come to pay respects at the shrine, or to draw attention to the saint on her holy day. Having said that, the June sighting this time was on the thirteenth rather than the fifteenth, although this could have simply meant the ghost got their date wrong!

Here concludes the second tour of the city, the busy Broadway is ahead of you and the High Street is to your left.

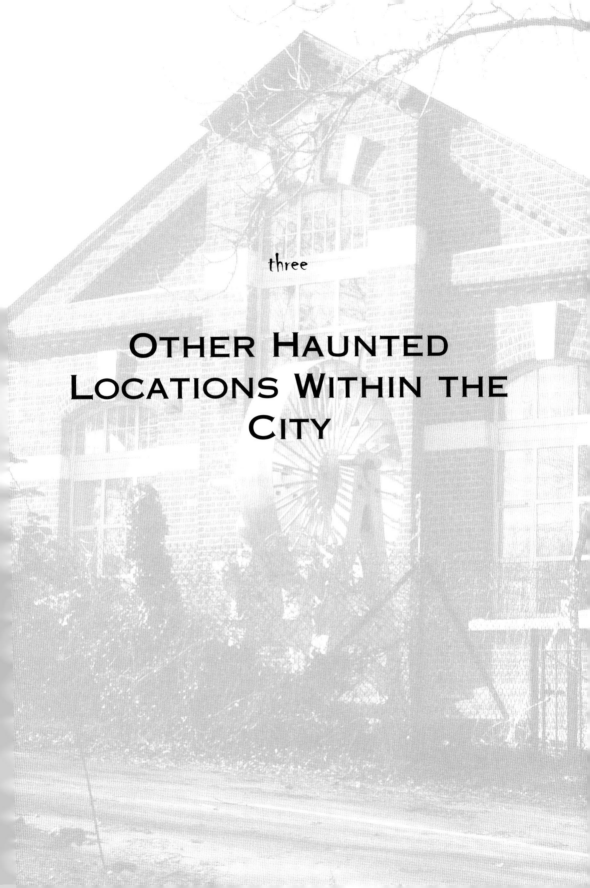

three

OTHER HAUNTED LOCATIONS WITHIN THE CITY

This chapter details the other supernatural events recorded within the city boundaries, in which I include the suburbs of St Cross, Weeke, Bar End, Badger Farm, etc. Thankfully there is a set of marker stones on each of the main roads out of Winchester which tell me where to stop! Each location comes with an Ordnance Survey grid reference which will make the identification of the haunting slightly easier.

Number 2, The Broadway (SU 485293)

On anyone's list of places which may be haunted, the premises of the local undertaker would feature quite highly. However, the strange experiences which have been reported at No. 2, The Broadway, have nothing to do with the undertaker's which now occupies the site but were witnessed a few years beforehand.

Number 2, from the 1980s to the mid-'90s was the location of one of Winchester's hardware stores and these stories were recounted to me by one of the owners, Mrs Donelly, in the back room of their new shop in St George's Street.

The hardware store was, like so many others of its type, cluttered and rather dusty. There was always the possibility that they might just have the oddment you were looking for or a host of other treasures hidden away. Many a time have I wandered in, intent on purchasing one thing only to leave with a multitude of other items which 'might be useful one day.' The stock in such a shop is always changing with demand for items fluctuating. As an example, one week there might be a run on 'Shellac,' as I found to my consternation a month or so ago, and when the product is reordered comes in a case of fifty. Never is there enough room on the shelf for all of these so the stock room get filled with the remainder until it too becomes part of the shop!

King Alfred the Great.

Such was the case with the back room of No 2, The Broadway.

To set the scene, this stock room also contained the back door of the then shop and by this stood a sink. By the sink was a chain attached to a staple in the wall; the reason for its location and use remaining lost to the mists of time. To the right of this was a doorway and staircase leading to an upstairs office and it was here, one day in the late 1980s, where Mrs Donelly was sitting and working.

Suddenly she started to realise that she was hearing a rhythmic drumming from below her. Cautiously she got up and started down the stairs to investigate the unusual noise. The chain, which normally hung lifeless and inanimate, as one would expect, was rocking backwards and forwards, and as it did so, hit against the sink producing the rapping. As she watched, it slowly stopped as though the force causing its movement had left the area. She did not ever witness or hear the chain move again while she worked at those premises, though several other strange things happened around that spot.

The back door of the shop was opened by a push-bar, which could only be opened from the inside and only then with considerable force. Attached to it was a strong spring so that it would close firmly behind anyone entering or leaving by it so as to deter would be thieves from entering or exiting by this door. One evening, at the end of the day, while Mrs Donelly was getting stock inside, she passed through the door with a heavy load and heard the door slam shut behind her. As she walked forward a few yards she heard the door open and slam again. Putting down her load she went to investigate since she believed that she was the only person working in that area of the shop. Since no one had entered it was only logical to suppose that somebody or something had left the building, yet she was not surprised when she could not find anything or anybody outside.

On another occasion, a wire, hung above the sink to dry tea towels and cloths, was found to be vibrating at an alarming rate; for which no logical explanation could be found. Mrs Donelly watched in hypnotic amazement for sometime before the clothes line became still again. All these experiences were one-offs and were not repeated to her knowledge. According to the receptionist of the undertaker's nothing strange has been witnessed since then, although it is to be noted that all these experiences happened within a few feet of each other in an area described by a later shop assistant as 'strange and unhappy.'

One final incident happened a few years before the store relocated when a part-time assistant saw something unusual in another part of the shop. Described by Mrs Donelly as a very level-headed young man who went on to become a lawyer, this assistant was standing on the till, which was sited by the front windows of the shop, looking down into the darker interior. It was quiet and there were no customers, but something drew his attention to the far left corner where he thought he glimpsed a lady, dressed in dark clothes with a black veil. Not having noticed her come in he went down the furthest aisle where he thought her to be. She was not there. Nor was she in any other aisle, nor out the back, nor had the bell on the door rung to signify her exit.

That part of the shop is now occupied by a high class interior designer, who was probably more surprised at me entering his premises (I am not the sort of person who looks as though he'll buy a high class kitchen) than to learn of possible supernatural occurrences happening around his polished chrome fittings!

I found Mrs Donelly to be a very sensible lady who would not be given to flights of fancy. She seemed genuinely interested in the supernatural while retaining a healthy scepticism based on the logic of reason. Yet she is aware of paranormal activity for one simple reason: she has experienced it first hand!

Number 45 Quarry Road (SU 494293)

It is not often that council houses are reported as being haunted and never to the extent described at this dwelling. For a number of years strange things of every paranormal type have been recorded here: apparitions, poltergeists, noises, smells, lights and more! The stories have become absorbed into local legend and a number of tales, which I shall recount here, have been used to illustrate other strange occurrences around the city. The haunted house attracted much media interest during the 1970s when the hauntings were at their highest and several perplexing events, or side-effects of events, were captured on camera. Before these houses were built the land was effectively a nondescript part of the field system of the area and nothing untoward happened here, as far as I can tell, prior to the building of them; the rest of the local ghosts tend to site themselves on St Giles Hill. I am indebted to several local residents of the Highcliff area, who prefer to remain anonymous, for much of the following information – they know who they are!

The Bowles family – husband, wife and four sons – moved into the council-owned house during 1968. Prior to their arrival nothing odd had been reported as having taken place nor had the family ever thought much about the supernatural, until…

The first thing that let the family know they had trouble was when things started disappearing and then re-materialising in different places; this poltergeist had a penchant for knives and kitchen utensils. Larger objects such as books would suddenly drop off tables and the occasional 'cold spot' would be felt. Sometimes, according to one local resident, a 'shimmering little disk' could be seen – could this be an early mention of what is now loosely termed an 'orb?' (See the item on St Catherine's Hill for a detailed description of what an orb might or might not be)

Mrs Bowles, who always seemed to be the centre of the paranormal attention, heard, early in 1969, her name being continuously called, and, according to her testimony, she would end up running from room to room trying to discover where the voice was calling from. Eventually she decided that she was becoming or had become mentally unstable and sought medical advice. The doctor, unable to locate anything wrong, suggested that she talked her problems over with the rest of her family. When she started to describe what was happening to her to her husband and children they too concurred with her since they were witnessing similar things themselves!

The turning point from when these activities were interesting to when they were unpleasant happened one night when Mr Bowles was working nightshift. Mrs Bowles was asleep in bed when suddenly she found herself brought very quickly to full consciousness; there were footsteps, loud and regular, pacing around her bed. Suddenly she felt as though she was being lifted out of her bed while at the same time she felt a large weight press down upon her chest. Her terror was further increased when the room was plunged into total darkness – it was even as though the streetlights outside had been extinguished! Suffice to say that it was many hours before she summoned up enough courage to take her head out from under the covers!

From then on disturbances of ever-increasing magnitude harassed the house and occupants, especially Mrs Bowles. Family and visitors alike would report strange, rotten smells and over time the smell of rotten eggs would herald the arrival of a regular figure dressed entirely in black. Instantly recognisable, this figure could date from the Victoria/Edwardian era and is distinguished from any other 'men in black' by long hair, whiskers, and cloak; the latter fastened by a brass chain and hook. As an aside, I have such a garment and when I lived near Quarry Road it was my ambition to dress up as this apparition and see if I could terrorise the neighbourhood! This ghost, although able to appear anywhere in the house, seldom moved but rather tended to look directly at the witness. One morning during the early 1970s, the next door neighbour of the Bowles was in the house talking over a cup of tea. As she got up to go she found that she was literally rooted to the spot for some unapparent reason. While she did not see anything at this time, Mrs Bowles, rushing to her aid, noticed the man in black standing just beside her. Once the apparition had vanished, after some seconds, the neighbour's legs became instantly free again.

After the man in black, the next most frequent visitor to the house was a typical black nun. This visitor was a very solid entity, unlike the man in black who tended to go hazy around the legs, and was apparently quite young. The haunt of this apparition was at the top of the stairs on the landing and always looking down on a person about to ascend the stairs. While one hand hung down by her side the other was stretched out and pointing towards the landing window.

The woman in white was also a frequent visitor around the house, a solid material form which in any other haunted location would be described in minute detail. During all this time the poltergeists were busy with their activities. They had a fiendish delight in throwing books about and heaving heavy brass candlesticks at strangers. Cold, clammy hands would be felt and on one occasion a friend of the family distinctly felt her hair being stroked by something unseen. The powerful bad smells were complemented by that of violets and the occasional orb was also seen, usually in conjunction with an odour. Lights also became part of the repertoire of the house and Mrs Bowles had a very vivid experience one night of such supernatural illumination. The clock had just chimed midnight and a hush enveloped the house whereby even the smallest of noises were multiplied and magnified. Suddenly she found herself wide awake and sitting upright in bed listening to her name being called. Slowly before her she became aware of a glow which expanded both in size and luminosity until it resembled a great shimmering cross of light. She watched intently for a few minutes before the form began to fade away from her again. Once more there was not much sleep to be had that night.

A favourite type of activity within the house became that of furniture moving. Occasionally accompanied by peculiar noises the furniture in any room could, with no advance warning, begin to move or levitate. It was the milkman who first witnessed the moving of one particular chair in the living room; prior to then all furniture moving was confined to the bedrooms. He had finished his round and was enjoying a cup of tea courtesy of Mrs Bowles when suddenly he ran out of the house. Later enquiries revealed that he had seen one of the chairs in the living room lift about an inch off the floor before dropping down again. Thinking it was a trick of his eyes he thought no more about it and carried on drinking his tea. To his horror the same chair suddenly took off along one side of the room before being set down facing the wall. In terror he fled!

After the first exorcism failed to rid the house of its now unwanted guests the media began to get interested. Several documentaries were made on location and the house stared to receive visits from the eminent ghost hunters of the day. The poltergeists would often annoy reporters by turning on or off their equipment and any lights they wanted to use. Electrical equipment of any type was fair sport when the outside broadcast crew were visiting!

Most of the stories detailed above appear fantastic even for a book on the supernatural and not surprisingly much has been written disproving these stories and discrediting Mrs Bowles. I present a selection of them here to allow the reader to make up their mind for themselves. Personally I feel that this haunting is like so many popular television programs of today on the subject. No matter what, the medium has to say something or something has to happen, if only to keep the viewers interested and wanting to tune in to the following episode. However, within most of these programs there is usually a sizable grain of truth which requires further investigation and I think the same can be said for No. 45 Quarry Road. On the other hand, if my sceptical nature can be proved wrong we have here a most interesting and unprecedented case.

The house was pulled down in 1987 for a new development and the new 'No. 45' stands nowhere near the haunted example; I therefore ask you not to trouble the residents.

And I haven't even touched on the other events that were supposed to have happened here: the face at the window beckoning, the footsteps in the kitchen, the flying tablecloths, the vibrating window catch…

Badger Farm to Compton (SU 464274 to SU 460259)

There is, or rather was, a persistent story attached to the ancient footpath which leads from the southern end of Badger Farm to the quiet hamlet of Compton. Before the current sprawl of uninspiring housing engulfed the ridge of Compton Down, the ghost of a monk, sometimes walking or most often riding a horse, has been observed heading down to Compton End. The last time this ghost was sighted was just after the Second World War so I think it can be classified as an historical haunting.

The reports of this haunting manifestation state that it is usually late at night, and always after sundown, when the sound of horse's hooves can be heard galloping at speed towards the unwary walker. As the horse and rider pass by the distinctive shape of a monk's habit can be discerned. The apparition, despite appearing to be quite solid, although not entirely material, disappears abruptly at the moment the bystander registers that there is something unnatural about the horse. Perhaps, since it gives the impression it has been cut off at the knees, this ghost follows an earlier, lower path which is about eighteen inches below the current surface.

The reason why this night-time ride takes place or who travels upon the horse remains a mystery locked up in the annals of time. And I doubt we shall ever find out.

The Bell Inn, St Cross (SU 475278)

Situated in the delightful hamlet of St Cross, near the ancient Hospital of St Cross (well worth a visit), the Bell Inn retains all the feeling of a quiet country pub. This is a friendly and welcoming place which consistently serves fine food and superb beer. When walking along the water meadows or visiting the nearby Hospital of St Cross, I can not recommend a better stopping place.

The supposed haunting that takes place here concerns one small part of the public bar where people often feel a sense of sadness or depression. A former barmaid was convinced that she saw a shadowy figure move across the area and had heard tapping similar to a gentleman's cane rapping on the flagstone floor. As with every cellar in the city, the odd crash has been heard originating from its depths for which there has been no explanation…

I have often watched those standing at this particular area of the pub and have noticed that those standing there are usually less cheerful than others elsewhere in the pub and that should they move to another position their mood almost always changes.

As far as I can make out there is no real reason why this should be the case. There have been no reports of anything untoward happening here although this is an ancient site with a great deal of history.

City bridge, where a miracle of St Swithun took place.

City Bridge (SU 485 292)

Within the annals of local legend comes another story pertaining to the miracles of the great city prodigy, St Swithun.

One of the great achievements of Swithun was the formation of trade and commerce within the city, turning it from a shambling collection of ruinous cottages to a bustling place of business. While trade from the west by land was achievable and from elsewhere by water the area to the east was effectively cut off from the city by the river. Swithun set about rectifying this by building, as part of the new defences to the city, a fine bridge of five spans of sufficient strength to carry the heaviest loads of the time. According to the inscription on the present bridge it seems to have taken Swithun's workmen eleven years to complete the bridge! However, they must have done a good job since it was 950 years before it was replaced and according to an excavation in the 1880s several of the arches remain buried under the current road surface. As an aside this excavation also revealed much of the medieval quay system including rope burns in the stone where boats had been moored.

Swithun, so we are told, liked to oversee much of the work of his projects personally. While his masons toiled he would watch what was happening, giving comment where required. One day while he inspected the bridge a poor peasant woman carrying a basket of eggs stumbled over a roughly hewn lump of stone which had been left on the path by a workman. Down went the basket and all the eggs inside were broken. Swithun, quite overcome with pity for the woman, bent down and picked up the basket. As he did so the contents were miraculously restored and she went on her way rejoicing.

Footsteps along the river (SU 486295 to SU 487287)

A curious phenomenon was noticed on 25 February 2003 by two people making their way from the bar end area of the city to a bridge near the Mash Tun public house (also haunted by a 'strange feeling' in the cellar – we will not dwell on this) on Eastgate Street. This rather strange occurrence lasted the entire journey, which was a distance of well over half a mile.

These two friends had set out on their journey at about 7.30 p.m. with the intent of visiting some other friends in another part of the city. Coming out of Milland Road and crossing over Chesil Street they were confronted with a set of what appeared to be wet footprints heading away towards the outskirts of the city. Remarking on how odd it was that someone had been walking with what seemed to be wet trainers they thought little more about it. It was only when they had got to the Chesil Theatre and the footprints were still fresh and distinct that they started to ask questions.

Postponing their visit they gave chase to the footprints. They crossed straight over the busy junction before heading along the passage between the youth hostel and the Cricketers (now sadly Blonde Beer Café). Emerging into Water Lane the footprints ran for a further hundred yards before moving to the path which runs alongside the river at this point. Still the footprints continued; they remained absolutely constant getting neither wetter nor dryer. Finally on one of the bridges, which links the lane with Eastgate Street they stopped abruptly. The friends searched the opposite bank for a while and the surrounding streets to see if they reoccurred anywhere else but to no avail.

When they returned to the bridge the prints were still on the decking so some testing was carried out. A handkerchief was used to wipe away some of the water, for testing later to see if it was an oil rather than water. Thinking it would be a good idea to see where the footprints finally led an expedition was launched to retrace the steps towards bar end. However, no sooner had they gone fifty yards then the marks began to fade. Within seconds they had all gone and the handkerchief, which had been wet through with the liquid was now bone dry.

When I was presented with the case I was more than a little intrigued. Given that these prints had been on the ground for at least half an hour with no sign of fading I found it difficult to believe that they would disappear in a few seconds if they were simply water. The handkerchief failed to respond to any tests I subjected it to and appeared to be perfectly normal and, surprisingly, clean! The night in question was cold but the temperature was well above freezing which rules out some of the questions on the longevity issue. The nature of the prints

Chesil Street, where a strange set of footprints were once seen.

themselves is also interesting. If somebody had fallen in the river and climbed out again I would have expected to find a puddle on the bridge deck; this was lacking according to the account. If this event had taken place sometime before the friends witnessed the footprints I would still assume that the initial footprints would be jumbled and indistinct. This was not the case – they were sharp and clear cut. This latter trait continued for the route of the occurrence. Under normal circumstances such a print would start very heavy and wet before diminishing as the water is dispersed. Even a heavily waterlogged trainer would not be able maintain such a print for half a mile.

The romantic ghost hunter in me surmises that somebody at some time fell off the bridge either by accident or design and was drowned in the river. Perhaps not realising or acknowledging their death they picked up on their journey where they left off and continued leaving only their ghostly wet footprints behind.

The Itchen Navigation, the River and the Water Meadows

In the not so distant past, up until the 1840s when the railway was built, Winchester had a bustling industry centred around the portion of the river known as the Itchen Navigation. For almost 2,000 years it was the main trading route into and out of the city. The Romans used it, as did Vikings during their raids, and during times of peace it was a place where courting couples used to wander. During both war and peace the medieval wealth achieved by the city came via the river.

Being bereft of any durable stone the major buildings have all been constructed using imported stone from the Isle of Wight, Purbeck and as far away as southern France – every block being brought up the river. Imagine too the grain and cloth trade, the throng of merchants bringing their wares to the annual St Giles' Fair, and the occasional royal barge bringing the monarch or visiting dignitary to the city. It was by this mode of transport that king Philip of Spain arrived during the heady days of July 1554 to visit for the first time, and to marry in the Cathedral the next day, Mary Tudor.

It is not surprising therefore that a number of chilling ghost stories have arisen along the length of this canal. Not all of them are genuine. For example, a legend was put around that a horse with flaming nostrils and striking sparks from its hooves would charge up the river at the dead of night turning all who looked at it mad with fright! This story was made up by the canal toll collector who enjoyed the revenue his monopoly generated. Unfortunately he also liked to sleep at night when toll evaders would sneak into the city. By playing on their superstitious nature he was able to protect his profit! The stories of the fiery horse ceased as abruptly as they began with the introduction of an Act of Parliament raised by the city's merchants which forbade the charging of additional tolls on the waterway!

Since the water meadows are a misty sort of place with a thick fog rising from them early in the morning or as the sun sets, especially in the autumn and winter months, ethereal shapes are frequently sighted. Most of these can be discounted; in the mist trees and other inanimate objects take on completely different forms and there is every possibility that the tall black-cloaked man carrying a flickering hurricane lamp is in reality your author wandering home from the pub! One story, however, is continually relayed by car drivers who have witnessed the phenomena along Garnier Road (SU 480281). They usually receive their surprise as they near a rather treacherous bend over a bridge near to the old sewage pumping station. Pieced together from all the reports I have heard, the following appears to happen:

Firstly a ball of white mist, between 5 and 10ft in diameter, rises from the southern side of the bridge – there are some sluices here – before setting down and crossing the road. The misty form then sets a course eastwards towards St Catherine's Hill, following a line roughly where the pavement meets the grass verge. At this stage it could remain as a large ball of mist or it could take on the vague outline of a woman in a long dress. Finally, never more than 30 yards, and certainly before it gets to the solitary house on the right, the spectre fades and disappears. The cause of this apparition is unknown, although there have been unconfirmed reports of a suicide taking place further upstream and the body then being fished out of the river at these sluices.

The following few stories are the best of a multitude which have been associated with this watery part of the city.

Where a bridge once stood and where an apparition still stands.

The Man on the Bridge (SU 484284)

At the time of writing there lie, almost hidden and practically forgotten, the remains of two bridge abutments which supported an arched wooden footbridge which used to span the waters about halfway between Tun Bridge and Wharf Bridge on the main Itchen navigation. It is here that a spectre of a man is said still to gaze down on the waters below, head bent in sorrow and contemplating the death of his family.

The story which was retold to me one dank and misty evening in October tells of the fate of a family almost 100 years ago. This part of the river is still very popular with boating types. The rowers of Winchester College practice daily during the summer months and those keen on their sport can be found making their way from their boathouse to the old lock under St Catherine's Hill and back even on the coldest of winter's days. I can only suppose that it was a custom, at the time when this story was set, for private craft to occasionally take to these waters and to enjoy a river trip and perhaps picnic under a shady willow which grows in proliferation along these banks. With the ducks, swans and other water fowl sharing the canal and the humble water vole cutting through the stream like a clockwork model, the warm afternoon sun setting on the ancient walls of the hospital of St Cross and the droning buzz of the dragonfly, I imagine that this place was, as it still near is, idyllic and perfect for such a expedition. But I digress.

This family party were out on the river in a small boat, the husband and wife and two small children. The details of what follows are not that exact, since there was no one else around to record the event, but for one reason or another – perhaps one of the children moved too suddenly, perhaps they hit the bank – the boat suddenly capsized and sank. Down went the upturned boat, under which the family struggled to get free. Although the river is quite shallow and slow moving it was only the husband who managed to swim out alive – the other three members of his family had been caught up in the long weeds which grow there and had been drowned.

For the next year the husband used to wander alone along the river past the spot where his family were killed, before standing on the bridge and pondering on the tragic accident it overlooked. It was there that they found him on the anniversary of the disaster, hanging from the railing with a rope around his neck.

From that time on observations of a ghostly watcher on the bridge used to be reported; staring simply at the slow-moving but murderous river below. It was said that a white mist could be seen at the same time as the ghostly apparition, marking the spot where the boat went down.

The bridge, being fundamentally rotten, was removed in the 1970s but even this fails to deter our ghost. In 1988 a woman walking her dog along the tow path from Garnier Road back towards the city received the shock of her life when, just as dusk was setting, she spied something odd above the river. Thinking it was a child's rope swing tied to the faithful oak which stands by the scene, she thought little of it, yet as she approached she noticed that it was larger and with more form than a length of rope; more like a pillar of swirling, translucent mist.

She stopped, or rather was stopped from progressing by her dog, which flatly refused to go any further, and watched. As she watched so it appeared that the apparition grew stronger. The head, torso, and finally the legs became more solid and she realised that she was looking at the pale figure of a man seemingly suspended, surreally, mid-air 10ft above the surface of the water. Unable to take the spectacle any longer she turned and with her dog ran back to Garnier Road.

The old chap who told me the above story is long dead and I have been unable to locate a report of the drowning or the hanging in the local press. Yet it remains a compelling tale. Although I have no other account of a full materialisation of this spectre, I have had several reports of a column of mist around or about the river within the vicinity of the old bridge. Could we have the return of a suicide, haunted by the loss of his family? Time, with further sightings, can only tell.

Garnier Road Pumping Station (SU 479282)

Half hidden in the trees about midway along Garnier road lies what used to be Winchester's sewage pumping station, now converted to a suit of luxury offices. There is a story told in the local pub for which I can find no external evidence and which I suspect was made up a number of years ago. However, it does make a good yarn…

Garnier Road station was used to pump Winchester's raw sewage. While the liquid was allowed to drain off into the river Itchen, the solid matter required pumping to the sewage farm behind St Catherine's Hill. Winchester's domestic rubbish was burned to raise steam and two large beam engines were employed in this smelly task. Before the more modern and now long-scrapped Sissons steam pumping engines were installed, there was an engine reputed to be haunted in quite an unusual way. Let us travel back in time to the end of the nineteenth century and visit the gas-lit pumping station late one night…

Garnier Road Pumping Station.

There had been a problem with one of the engines and it had stopped working. Since the problem was not that large the mechanic on duty shut the engine down and repaired the problem himself. This was quickly achieved and he got up, picking up his equipment as he did so. Staggering with the heavy tools he misjudged a step and fell backwards against a hot steam pipe. His arm, although not too badly burnt, was not treated and after a day or two the wound began to turn gangrenous. Within a week he was off work, seriously ill, and within two he had died from the infection that riddled his entire body.

From then on inexplicable occurrences started to happen at the pumping station. Objects, usually small tools, spanners, wrenches or pliers, used to disappear and reappear in odd inaccessible places. A favourite place for the ghost to return items was on the top of the engine beam. This is the highest part of the engine and is out of the reach of even the tallest person; it also moves quite dramatically when the engine is working. On one occasion it is said that some new boiler fittings mysteriously moved by themselves from the stores to a place high above the engine: they were so tightly wedged were they that they remained in that position until the engine was scrapped!

Mechanical problems also increased. It seemed that parts of the pumping plant started to go wrong more often; pumps would get blocked frequently and raising steam in the boilers was now always difficult. Work became harder for the men employed there and morale grew lower and lower. Conveniently, all these problems were blamed on the ghost of the unfortunate man who had died.

Over time it is usually found that a haunting diminishes and appearances become rarer and rarer: especially in the case of poltergeist incidents. However, instead of getting quieter over time the supernatural activities started to happen progressively frequently.

The climax came late one evening in November when the mechanic on duty began to hear that one of the bearings on the engine was starting to make an unusual noise. He immediately shut off the steam to the engine and it began to slow to a stop. Gathering up his tools he went to assess the problem. Everything appeared to be in order; the main bearing on the beam was fine, the others he could reach appeared to be all right too. Puzzled, he walked around the rest of the engine checking every part. Nothing appeared to be amiss. He then checked the valve gear motion. This is the most complicated part of the machine and relatively inaccessible.

Suddenly, as he was in the very innards of the engine, he heard some alarming sounds. Firstly there was the squeak of the steam valve followed by the heavy clunk of an engine operator lifting the valves to start the engine. With a shout he started to wriggle out of the confined space but it was by then too late; he was drawn into the massive workings and was crushed to death.

An hour later his colleague, who was working in the boiler house, wondering what had happened to his ten o'clock tea was surprised to find the door of the engine house locked. Worried, he immediately fetched a friend from his nearby house and between them broke down the door. The mangled remains of the engine operator were eventually removed from the workings once the engine had been persuaded to stop. Once the steam had been turned off it took a full ten minutes for the beam to finally slow to a halt.

It appears that from then on all was quiet at the pumping station. Seemingly, the death of another worker satisfied the malicious spirit that had been haunting the building.

The Spectral Hound (SU 483281)

The horse with the flaming nostrils and spark generating hooves may be a complete fabrication but many reports have come to light that over the years a ghost dog has been spotted running along the banks of the river. There are no hard and fast rules regarding this particular spectre except that it is most frequently sighted trotting along the former tow path to the immediate north of Tun Bridge on the west bank. I questioned one local dog walker, Sharon Lodge of Stanmore, during the latter part of December 2005 and she stated that she had witnessed the ghostly form of a dog less than a week before.

Having parked her car at the bottom of St Catherine's Hill she and her dog, Dizzy, set off for a quick walk and play along the river and through the fields owned by Winchester College. No sooner had they left the road and started along the muddy footpath a dog was spotted trotting towards them. Instantly Sharon's dog began to race towards the other dog, a golden Labrador; tail wagging in friendly welcome. Abruptly Dizzy stopped, her hackles raised, and a low growl issued from the now shaking animal. Sharon, expecting a fight, grabbed hold of Dizzy and prepared to fend off the other animal should it attack. The other dog kept on ambling towards her and, to her horror and surprise, looked as though it was passing through the clumps of grass rather than bounding over them. As it drew near its form became less and less distinct before fading away altogether less than five yards from the terrified pair.

The bounding spectre of a dog runs along the path here.

That was the end of that day's walk and they have not taken that particular route since, preferring to keep at least the river between them and any ethereal dog.

Their story is not unique although probably one of the most developed. A retired couple walking the same route a year ago heard the pant of an approaching dog at speed and moved to one side of the path to let it pass. They saw nothing but distinctly felt an animal brush past them as it went on its way. Another time, admittedly a few years ago, a family having a picnic had to pack up in a hurry after chasing away a stray dog that was troubling them; for as they chased it so it faded away!

Jolly Farmer (SU 477304)

Not such a jolly place this. It was here that the city used to site its gallows and the stench of death lingers on. Invariably it is grey and wet when I venture to this part of the city; I try not to stay on this hill longer than I have to. That aside, the Jolly Farmer pub, a Giant's Plate restaurant, is a very welcoming place where I have enjoyed several good meals over the years.

Here also is the spirit of an executed man, Henry Whitley, who causes a fair amount of poltergeist activity. It is said that he committed the capital crime of stealing seven hens in 1637 and was executed by the hangman's noose within a day of the guilty verdict being passed down.

Henry has since been known to cause all kinds of mischief. A much-loved trick which has been recorded since the pub was built involves turning on water taps and at least one insurance claim for a flood has had the cause of incident as 'supernatural'! Even quite large objects such as a glass washer have been moved and when I spoke to some regulars in there a couple of years ago I was assured that their poltergeist was still very active.

Kingsgate Road (SU 478284)

On 25 February (note that the date is the same as the 'footsteps along the river') many years ago a young man and his dog set off for Basingstoke by car from his mother's house in Kingsgate Road. It was snowing hard and before too long he had managed to slide it very neatly into a ditch. Unharmed he flagged down a passing detachment of soldiers from the barracks making their way into the city and after promising to give them a ride into town they lifted his car back onto the road, setting off with haste. The preamble to this story has nothing to do with the ghostly occurrence that took place later on, suffice to say the inability to get to Basingstoke led to the young man returning back to his mother's house where he spent the night.

Since he had not resided at that address for some time there was no bed made up for him; however, his mother gave up her room and he and his dog settled down for the night there. It was not to be a peaceful or, for that matter, a restful night since at 2.00 a.m. he was awoken by a frantic banging and crashing emanating from the wardrobe. The dog's hackles were up; growling and barking at the strange and unseen noise. An investigation of the wardrobe showed that there was nothing to account for the noise and a watchful vigil was kept on the door until morning. The young man, recounting his experience to his mother the following morning, was surprised to learn that she had heard it many times and it was nothing at all out of the ordinary!

The Rising Sun

Situated just outside of the city walls in the area known as the Soke, the Rising Sun can be found by heading due east along the High Street until you start to climb Magdalene Hill. Interestingly the word *soke* has nothing to do with 'soak' or to make wet, despite this being a very damp portion of the city. Rather it is an old word which means 'at liberty' and the bishops of Winchester were 'at liberty' to do what ever they wished with this land and those who lived on it!

Over the years the Rising Sun has been the scene of many strange happenings – not all of them authentic. Some stories have been made up to encourage questioning, while in the past few years any reports of the supernatural have been dismissed by the owners. However, on with the chronicle of Winchester's hauntings.

It was here during the Civil War, when Winchester was in the hands of the Royalists, that Cromwell's men were imprisoned in the cellar: their marks can be seen and heard to this day. While we would all expect to hear the sounds of tortured soldiers groaning in their chains here we are also treated to some supposed mysterious blood stains appearing from time to time upon the dungeon wall.

At one time poltergeist activity was the order of the day down here too! Beer barrels have been found overturned and out of their racks while other objects have been thrown about in the presence of former tenants and their customers. One of the most inexplicable events took place a few years ago when some money had disappeared out of a locked safe. It was not so much the disappearance that baffled the authorities rather the reappearance of the money a short time later in another part of the pub which had previously been searched a few minutes before. This incident happened on more than one occasion and additional security measures were implemented. The safe was protected by an independent alarm, a time switch and an infra-red motion detector – still the money would disappear and reappear elsewhere.

Another of the tunnels which runs through the city rises in the cellar of the pub, revealing its ancient foundations. It was supposed to have run under the river to the Cathedral or Wolvesey Palace. Alas it is unlikely that we shall ever know since the portion under the river collapsed many years ago and further falls now make it only a few yards long.

If you have the courage to stay at this hostelry it also provides bed and breakfast accommodation. However, it is best to avoid staying in Room 3 if at all possible. It is reported that an unearthly presence is felt in that room and anyone who tries to spend a night there will be dogged by bad dreams and a sense of unease which even copious amounts of drink cannot dispel.

The Royal Hotel (SU 481295)

More clerics! The city seems to be full of spectral monks and nuns! One is led to wonder, with all the ghostly apparitions of monks, whether any have ever joined the choir celestial. This is yet another spot in the middle of the city where a ghostly procession appears to make their muttering way from the hotel to the High Street. The current hotel was built on the site of one of the numerous medieval convents and the slow chant of prayer has been heard here for at least a century. The receptionist was rather cool about the haunting though – nothing has ever occurred to her knowledge.

The Royal Hotel with its procession of monks and nuns.

St Catherine's Hill (SU 484276)

One could wax lyrical about this place for thousands of words and still not give it the descriptive justice it deserves; even the most staid writer becomes romantically poetic when recounting their experiences here. However, since this is not a guide book or a historical treatise (as I constantly have to remind myself) but rather an exposition of the supernatural of the city I shall have to content myself with providing just the bare specifics of the hill.

The shape and structure of the hill as we see it today derives, in the main, from its occupation as a fort during the Iron Age. The great ditches can still be seen and traced with ease and we can imagine will little difficulty the stockades and round houses that once held the population here safe from the ravages of invaders and wolves. Evidence survives for a continued occupation right up to the Norman period, for during this time a chapel was built on its summit to a peculiar design more at home in the Austrian alps than in the rolling hills of Hampshire. Cut in the top of the hill before the trees is a mysterious 'Miz-maze.' Its purpose and date are a matter of contention although most agree that it probably dates from the Middle Ages with periodical re-cutting to keep the turf from swallowing it up. It is not a maze as we tend to think of them today; it is a continual ribbon which starts to the southern side and finishes in the middle. Similar have been found around the country and abroad with explanations stating that they could be used as an aid to meditation or as a penance by monks – it bears striking resemblance to something similar in Chartres Cathedral. Local legend tells of a boy from Winchester College who, unable to return home, came up to the hill and cut it before dying (*See* Winchester College). The Pagan explanations, both modern and ancient, are numerous and are worth a study in their own right.

Whatever the purpose of the maze it is a very good place to practice dowsing with rods. Carefully walk from one edge of the maze to the other, not treading on the delicate turf around the route of the labyrinth, watching all the while the ends of your rods. With a couple of passes you will be able to determine two lines of 'energy' running in a George Cross fashion over the maze. One runs from the gap in the earth bank and away to the south while the other follows what is known as the 'Winchester Ley.'

The latter is an imaginary line which starts at Tidbury Ring and passes in a straight line through a long barrow, St Bartholomew's church, Hyde Abbey, the Lady Chapel in the Cathedral (which was the site of a Roman temple and Cenwalh's first Cathedral), and the maze on St Catherine's Hill before terminating at a tumulus. First noted by Alfred Watkins, who discerned that ancient sites ranging from crossroads to hill forts were invariably were linked by straight lines, these leys have become, in recent years, more connected with the study of energy lines in the earth and the search for spirituality.

The hill contains several legends, which is not surprising given its prominent position over the city and its various uses over the millennia. At Mottistone Common, on the Isle of Wight, there stands the Long Stone which legend tells was thrown there by a giant from St Catherine's Hill. In local Arthurian folklore a dragon was supposed to have appeared above the hill foretelling the birth of King Arthur to the wizard Merlin. In later times the dragon was supposed to live in a cave in among the Dongas, which are ancient cattle droves resembling narrow valleys, although with the construction of the M3 through this area and Twyford Down I suspect the dragon is now long gone.

Plague Pit Valley is the aptly named depression to the south of St Catherine's Hill. It was here that the dead of Winchester were buried when the plague struck. Mass graves were dug and barges full of the deceased victims would be brought to this spot for interment. For the centuries that followed this area was a place of foreboding and dislike. Even twenty years ago when the plan to build the motorway through Winchester was first mooted, the cheap option of following the old bypass route and then skirting up this valley was rejected, for fear of disturbing the virus of the plague!

Nearby Twyford Down, so I have been informed from a former road protestor, is the alleged site of a curse according to some. In 1992 when the motorway was being constructed, the graves of eighteen 'giants' were discovered. When a couple of unfortunate deaths took place the protesters immediately claimed that an ancient curse had caused them to happen.

The hill is also host to a strange occurrence whereby a visitor is treated to the feeling of being surrounded by a warm wind. This 'warm spot' – the distinct opposite to the more often reported 'cold spot' – tends to move around the crown of the hill allowing the individual to step in and out of its protection. It is as though the natural wind here is unable to penetrate some form of invisible barrier.

Within the trees at the top a legend has sprung up stating that the figure of a suicide who was found hanging on one of the beech trees a few years ago returns to the spot of their death. Several sightings of 'orbs' have been witnessed here as well.

The 'orb' is a fascinating thing. Prior to the age of digital recording and compact cameras it was very rarely witnessed. It is a common belief that an orb is the first stage of a physical manifestation of a spirit of some form or another. While some moving images can be quite convincing – dancing orbs with fluttery innards – the majority of still images I have viewed are no more than dust particles reflected in the lens of the camera. I have noted that most orbs appear in dusty places or indoors. A good number of these have been put to me as conclusive evidence not only for the existence of orbs but also for the reality of the spirit life. The close proximity of a flash to a modern lens and the nearness of the lens to the sensor of a digital camera is probably the cause of most orbs. A conventional 35mm SLR or digital SLR will very rarely produce an orb! Having rubbished most 'orb' pictures some I have viewed are quite spectacular and could be some form of energy, much in the same way as ball lightning and will o' the wisps have been reported over the years.

One of the more interesting occurrences which has happened on the hill in recent years came about during a 'ghost tour' I was conducting for a group of colleagues one evening in January. I had taken them around the water meadows and the lower end of the city and was just about to call it a night and head home. Unfortunately I made some glib comment about the legends of the hill, the myriad of ghosts that could be found en route and the wonderful view of the city illuminated at night. The next thing I knew we were setting off up the long steep path from the car park to the top of the hill. On arriving at the top we promptly scared a group of young scouts who were undertaking some night-time activity in the trees at the summit, this was hardly surprising since we were all dressed in dark clothing and carrying oil lamps – terrified, they thought that we were ghosts!

I started waxing lyrical about the history and the pre-history of the hill, the Iron Age and the ley lines, the warm spots and the dragon, while the members of the group exhausted and shivering feigned wrapt attention. Just at the right moment a 'warm spot' enveloped us and most people were able to feel a difference in temperature, which is always a relief, and they were able to walk in and out of it. We followed this phenomenon around the edge of the hill for a few minutes before I stopped to tell them some noteworthy bit of irrelevant information about the construction of the Hospital of St Cross which we were directly above.

Abruptly the atmosphere on the hill changed. Whereas one second all was jovial, the next this had been replaced by a still calm of intense foreboding; the hill itself seemed to become

St Catherine's Hill with its many and various apparitions.

darker and threatening. Some other members of the party felt it too, while others were blissfully unaware of the sudden change which had taken place. I became aware of a force, unseen and unfelt, emanating from the very top of the hill. The pricking of the hairs on the back of my neck told me that we should no longer be where we stood – we had outstayed our welcome.

As quickly as I could, ably aided by my assistant, I led the reluctant group to the steps on the south side before bringing them down the hill. There are a great number of steps here and they need to be attempted with caution, especially in the dark, since they are all of unequal length and height. However, by the time we reached the bottom we were all running. My assistant, who was following the party down, later reported that she had felt something literally push her all the way. She slammed the gate leading onto the footpath and we all stopped to recover.

At the debriefing meeting held in the pub half an hour later we were all sure that we had been involved in something out of the ordinary. Our various versions of events recall that most people had felt something strange at the hill and that by the time we reached the bottom all were aware of something not being quite 'right'. One person glimpsed something that resembled a group of people with flaming torches and another remarked that they had received a series of prods in the back during the descent.

I have been up on the hill many times since then, including at night, and yet have never experienced anything like that night since. It remains something of a mystery as to what happened on that night or what the cause was. Had we or the scouts before us done something to upset the spirits of the place? Were we caught up in a ghostly re-enactment? What ever it was it was certainly one of the most interesting nights, from a paranormal position, in my life which I hope never to experience again!

Tunnels under the city

I should imagine that this subject alone could fill an entire book. The tunnels, which at one time riddled the city, are frequently talked about but locations remain sketchy. In the interest of security I have been requested by the shop in question, which hosts an entrance to a very well preserved passageway, to keep the location a secret.

I was generally being annoying and pestering a shop assistant about possible haunting manifestations in her shop in August 2005. She called her manager to get me evicted but to her horror discovered that the manager and I had been the best of friends at college some years earlier. Consequently I was able to get full access to subterranean parts of the building in which predictably characteristic strange sounds had been heard.

On descending the rickety wooden stairs to the first part of the cellar one is immediately met with the chill air of foreboding. This is further heightened when, passing through the old sales stands and dead stock, we stumble down a few stone-cut steps into a large and disused room with its ceiling supported by strong arches. This forgotten place could be medieval, or Norman, or Saxon, or Roman; impossible to tell in the faint light of my torch. Behind a piece of plywood boarding on one wall is the tunnel. Being about 5ft high with a width of just under 3ft I squeeze myself in. Bent double and constantly hitting my hard-hatted head on the ceiling I inch along a few yards. I don't know in which direction I'm going but I do know that I am now at a junction. One passage leads to another cellar in another shop, so I am informed, while the other leads towards the Cathedral. I press on into the very bowels of the city for a fair way before meeting with a barrier of rubble, rubbish and waste. This is where the roof had fallen in, although I suspect, looking at the detritus, that this has been placed here purposefully. It is also here that chilling sounds have been heard.

Speaking to the manager he reported that when – with trepidation – he investigated the tunnel for the first time he was constantly aware of someone or something behind him. Whenever he moved, he heard an echo and when he stopped to listen, the echo also stopped. Having tested the acoustics down there I can confirm that in no portion of the passage can an echo be created. When he got to the blockage he was confronted with the sound of scratching and scrabbling. Not wishing to scare himself any more than he needed he decided that the origin of the noise was local rats.

Realising that there was no way forward he started to ease himself back along the way he had come. All of a sudden he heard the sharp sound of iron on stone. Thinking he had kicked something he looked about him; there was nothing except the powdery chalk floor. He heard the noise again, but this time twice in quick succession followed by a loud guttural cough. This proved too much for his nerve and turning round in the tunnel he ran as fast as he could back to his own cellar. The next day he nailed the entrance up and no one, living at least, visited the tunnel until I did a year or so later.

The only remaining trace of the White Horse Inn; even the ghost has gone.

As a supernatural investigator I have to report that I failed to hear anything during my visit to the passage. The story that the store manager told was nevertheless persuasive; he had certainly heard something on his one and only visit down there. He, at least, is convinced the tunnel is very much haunted.

The White Horse (SU 481294)

It has been many years since this building was a pub but the tale of the ghost in the White Horse was recounted to me, as so many stories have been, in another of the city's numerous drinking places.

By all accounts a ghost of a young girl is said to haunt the staircase, where she was seen from time to time right up to the closure of the premises. Descriptions of her differ, as do the feelings reported by those who suppose to have seen her. Some say that she is a happy child while others say that she appears to be overcome by uncontrollable grief.

The story goes that she was a servant girl in the employ of the establishment and was wickedly used and overworked by the landlord. Some say that she accidentally tripped and fell down the stairs while bringing down a laundry basket which was too heavy for her. Others say she threw herself down them in a mad, terminal attempt to be free of her employer. And still others state that the spiteful landlord pushed her down them. All stories converge to say that when she landed at the bottom her neck was broken and from that time on she was doomed to haunt the stairway forever.

One old gentleman informed me that a, 'regular, alcoholic gentleman, of poor repute, if you understand,' saw her sitting on the stair one evening, went 'mad' overnight and signed the pledge the next day – he never touched a drop of beer again!

All has been quiet since the pub has closed and a number of internal changes have taken place. It appears that 'forever' lasted, thankfully, less than 100 years.

Winchester Castle (SU 478294)

There is little left to see of the original fortified stronghold at the top of the city. With the exception of the Great Hall everything else was razed by Charles II to form a new royal palace. Plans still exist for the great building and formal grounds which were to be the envy of the royal households of Europe. Greatly influenced by Versailles, Charles wanted to clear the city of inhabitants and buildings for the most part and create a magnificent avenue down the hill to the west door of the Cathedral. Thankfully the monarch died and with him the ill-conceived idea. During his life he did, however, rebuild the castle into a well-proportioned palace, but even that, alas, was destroyed by a fire in the late nineteenth century. Used as a military barracks for 300 years it had now been turned into a bespoke set of flats. The military museums within the complex are, however, well worth a visit.

As mentioned in the above paragraph only the Great Hall survives. This must be one of the most awe-inspiring secular buildings to have survived. Built between 1222 and 1235 it reflects the changing tastes from the heavy Norman architecture to the soaring arches of the Early English Gothic style. It was used for the assizes off and on until as recently as 1974 when the hideous monstrosity now tacked on to its eastern end was built.

Its most interesting item of furniture contained within the building is the Round Table. Legend ascribes it to the court of King Arthur yet the historian dates it to the thirteenth century. Brilliantly painted, it carries the representation of Henry VII as King Arthur. The former had it repainted during the early years of his reign – the fascination with the Arthurian legend is nothing new, not even in Tudor times. The table was probably built by Edward I in about 1270, who saw himself at that time as the new 'Arthur'.

Besides the Round Table and the myriad of myth and legend in which it is enveloped, there is one other tale relating to the Great Hall which is worth retelling here. During the reign of Edward the Confessor the castle was used as a royal palace for much of the year and this event is reputed to have happened during an evening meal. On bringing some portion of the meal to the high table one of the servants slipped and then managed to regain his balance. This unremarkable scene was observed by the King and Earl Godwin, who ventured to make a light joke on the matter, that in reference to the servant's legs, 'that one brother support the other.' Edward, bristly and humourless at the best of times, was quick to reply that he should have been assisted by his brother, Alfred, had not Earl Godwin prevented it. The Earl, jumping to defend himself and to free himself of his involvement with the murder of Alfred, stated as a trial that if the accusation were true then the next morsel he consumed would be his last. He ate and swallowed, the bread became stuck in his throat and he choked. He fell dead under the table.

It is not surprising that the dungeon of Winchester Castle carries a few stories for it has seen some curious events over the centuries. It was here that Henry III cast a jury in to the 'lowest dungeon of the castle' as they would not deliver the verdict required on thirty highwaymen who had been brought to trial. Those condemned and those condemning were all friends so it is not unexpected that there was a disinclination to make use of the gallows!

Another story concerns an incident around the 1600s when it is said that the devil appeared to four women prisoners who were incarcerated there at the time on more than one occasion. It was reported that he came to the windows like a fire and shook the bars violently and that at another time like 'a great black thing with great eyes.' When the prisoners screamed the gaoler came running but failed to see anything except some strange physical anomalies. One of the candles he was carrying burnt dim before going out while another burnt with a blue flame. He also noted that the devil had left 'an unsavoury odour' in the room where the prisoners were kept. Nothing like this had been reported before and nothing similar since.

One of the more gruesome executions which has taken place at Winchester Castle involves that of Walter de Scoteneye (Scotney in today's spelling). He was condemned for the murder of Walter de Clare and of the attempted murder of his brother, Richard de Clare, 6th Earl of Hertford and 2nd Earl of Gloucester, in 1259 and died in a novel manner.

The manor of Crowhurst was owned by the Fitz-Lambert family until the later half of the thirteenth century when it passed to Walter de Scoteneye, who fought on the third crusade with Richard. On his return he was found guilty of the murder and attempted murder at a trial in the Great Hall. His sentence was to be torn apart by horses and the gruesome spectacle that followed is said to have been spectrally replayed several times during the year after Scoteneye's death.

Winchester College (SU 482289)

With a foundation in the fourteenth century Winchester College is one of the oldest public schools in existence. It became the model for Eton and King's College and was unsurpassed in its day. Founded by the great William of Wykeham, of whom we read of at the Cathedral, it can still boast that the majority of its medieval buildings still stand and are used for the exact purpose they were intended.

The ghosts which are reputed to haunt the old buildings are almost all certainly the work of fiction; of the over imagination of the boys running riot. At the same time they may well have been put about to scare the younger members of the school or to keep people from staying out when they were not supposed to. Needless to say there abound gruesome tales of boys who have died in some horrific manner or another and whose wraiths have come back to haunt the building.

Legends also abound. As ever they conflict, contradict and overlap alarmingly, none more so that that of *Dolce Domum*, chanted on the evening preceding the Whitsun holidays. The story tells of a boy who was chained to a pillar for some misdemeanour and composed the song. The same boy is also said to be responsible for cutting the miz-maze at the top of St Catherine's Hill; perhaps causing the punishment of being lashed to a stone? In another version he is tied up and the *Domum* song is directed at him. Further confusing narrative recounts that a boy, unable to travel home during the vacation, sits under the *Domum* tree where he composes the work before dying of a broken heart. Finally we reach a story which states that a young man was chained to a tree during the holidays. With bitter tears he writes the song before going up the hill to cut the maze. On his way down he then drowns himself in the river … and having pored over many accounts of the legend to get one which is suitable for publication here I am tempted to follow his example!

The tower of Winchester College where a strange glow has been seen.

As regards actual hauntings the facts are a little unclear. The tower of the chapel seems to have had at least one observed hit by ball lightning or similar in the 1920s. The parallels between this case and that of the phenomena observed at Wolvesey Palace less than 100 yards away is quite striking. One now very elderly gentleman, walking along College Walk one evening after a storm, noticed bright against the still thunderous sky a large glow against the top of the tower. Thinking that there had been a lightning strike and that the place was possibly on fire he rushed as fast as he could to the gate house. As he rounded the corner into College Street the glow disappeared and there was no trace of damage on the tower or the rest of the building. At no time did he see any flame or smoke issuing from the structure.

The other quite well-recorded manifestation to be found at the College is that of a wraith of a small child standing outside of the gatehouse in College Street. Contemporary reports state that the apparition is frequently glimpsed reflected in the headlamps of a passing car and is gone in an instant. Descriptions tend, therefore, to be vague, largely imprecise and usually conflicting. However, pieced together accounts reveal that a child can be seen to the immediate right of the gate, dressed in drab coloured clothes and with an untidy mess of light blond hair. I managed to track down one witness to this spirit who had almost crashed his car in reaction to it in October 1992. At the interview I posed the question which has been uppermost on my mind since first hearing the story some years ago, that the ghost could be nothing more than the shadow of a concrete bollard which appears in the exact spot that the apparition has been sighted? The answer I received, strong and forceful in the extreme, stated in no uncertain terms that not only could the child be seen by the car driver but so could the bollard – through the child!

The why and wherefore of this ghost remain a mystery too. There are no reports that I can find in any of the papers which shed any further light on this haunting.

Wolvesey Palace (SU 484290)

There is little of the original Wolvesey still to see here, although the ruins of the castle built during the twelfth century are quite striking. This castle and bishop's palace has been expanded over the years and during times of war and peace has seen some interesting spectacles. It was here that Mary Tudor first met Philip of Spain prior to their marriage in Winchester Cathedral the next day and it subsequently became a frequent stopping place for royalty during the Middle Ages.

With fortified palaces passing out of fashion in the 1600s the then owner, Bishop Morley, decided to have a house built alongside. This became Wolvesey Palace and bishops of Winchester have continued to live there from time to time.

Unfortunately, architect Thomas Finch, who was a contemporary of Wren, made the medieval mistake of neglecting to incorporate any solid foundations under the building. The subsequent subsidence has resulted in the demolition of the north and west wings, leaving only what you see today. As part of the current palace the chapel from the medieval castle was incorporated. While the Bishop of Winchester continues to live in Wolvesey Palace the castle is now under the care of English Heritage.

Before we can comment on some of the strange thing reputed to have happened here we need to explore some of the history behind the place. The name, despite what many will tell you, probably derives from the Saxons. In the time of Edgar it was customary for the Welsh Prince to deposit some 300 wolves' heads annually on an island to the south of the ancient city. Such an island could quite conceivably be the Wolvesey we have today.

The great siege and battle of Winchester could also have led to some of the apparitions which have been witnessed in the locality. The whole story is long and involved but I shall endeavour to keep this rendition of it short.

King Stephen and Empress Matilda both wanted to be the supreme monarch of England. Each had rival claims on the throne and neither would submit to rule by the other. Hence a civil war ensued, with most cities, the church and the nobility becoming greatly embroiled. Winchester more than any other city bore the brunt of a vicious battle in 1141 because Stephen had installed his brother, Henry du Blois, as bishop — not that Henry was averse to changing sides as the mood took him! Finally, after much persuasion, Henry pinned his colours to the mast of Stephen. Matilda was, at this time, based in Winchester Castle and Henry, from his fortified palace at Wolvesey, was able to lay the castle to siege.

Matilda was fighting away from the city and when news arrived of the siege at Winchester Castle she immediately returned with reinforcements. Effectively a double siege then took place between the two parties. At this time Winchester was set on fire and many of the ecclesiastical institutions were burnt to the ground.

Matilda, realising that the battle was slowly starting to swing in the direction of Stephen, made plans for her escape. She arrived at a cunning plan whereby she would pretend to be dead, lull all into a false sense of security, and then restart the battle somewhere else when she had re-mustered her forces.

She ordered a lead-lined coffin to be delivered to the castle and hired in some professional mourners to add to the occasion before sending word to Henry that she had passed on. With great pomp and ceremony her coffin was brought out of Winchester Castle for the onlookers to see. One report of the occasion even states that Henry came back to the city to administer the last rites over the coffin as it made its way to Devizes.

Eventually Matilda lost the war, not that this was ever admitted as such, and she fled to Normandy. However, at the treaty of Wallingford Matilda's son Henry was named heir to the English throne after the death of Stephen. She may have won after all!

The Roundheads destroyed the building, along with many other castles, leaving it in the ruinous state we see it today. As L'Estrange remarks, 'the man who can call the ruins picturesque must have a happy imagination'.

Unsurprisingly there are a number of different ghosts reported hereabouts. In a mirror of what has been observed on the tower of Winchester College opposite, a mysterious ball of light has also been discerned lodged high up on the ruins. The cause of such a phenomenon is unknown but there are at least three cases similar to this in the locality which point to ball lightning.

Apparitions of people have also been noted within the ruins and in a wide variety of different styles of dress. One American tourist I had the pleasure of talking to last year was ecstatic at having witnessed his first ghost. Apparently he glimpsed the archetypical male figure in Tudor costume in an arched doorways set halfway up one of the internal walls. Others have reported seeing similar figures around the grounds. Always just a glimpse and nothing more.

One day during the summer of 1994 a local man was walking past the outside curtain wall which separates the palace and the ruins from the rest of the city at a point near The Weirs. He heard what he thought at the time was a particularly violent game of cricket or rugby coming from the other side of the fortification; this would not be unusual as The Pilgrims' School use the area as a playing field.

On passing the entrance gate he stopped and looked in expecting to see the boys playing. Much to his amazement and fear there was nobody there and the gate was locked. His nerve failed him as the sound died instantly away and he ran all the way to Kingsgate! Thinking back, as he recounted the tale some ten years later, the sound was nothing like that of sport. In what game do you hear the crash of iron on iron and the explosion of cannon? He is convinced that he overheard the traces of an earlier battle when the stakes were life or death. As he said at the interview, a centuries old battle is the last thing you expect to witness on a sunny Sunday afternoon!

four

HAUNTED PLACES
OUTSIDE OF THE CITY

As we have seen so far in this book there is a phenomenal amount of paranormal activity within the delightful (or perhaps not so delightful now you have read about its sordid past) city of Winchester. Within this chapter we shall expand our net to catch the cream – if you'll pardon the mixed metaphors – of supernatural activity in the outlying villages and quiet country places that define this part of Hampshire.

As ever the manifestations shall be reported in alphabetical order with a grid reference to aid identification.

Cheriton (SU 598292)

The vast battle that took place here during the Civil War is one which lives on, not only in the history books and re-enactment societies but in the form of ghostly soldiers returning to the place of great carnage where they met their death.

The Battle of Cheriton is one of the defining encounters of the Civil War. On 29 March 1644 the Royalists, under the leadership of Ralph Hopton, and the Parliamentarians, commanded by William Waller, set to in one of the boldest clashes of the war. Despite the day starting well for the King's men, the sheer weight of numbers from Waller's men meant that the victory was eventually his. This effectively stopped the march of the Royalists south-eastwards and became a turning point for the campaign.

In the years that followed, reports soon began to appear of the sound of battle being heard on the anniversary of the conflict. During the past century soldiers of both sides have been seen and heard, although there have been no details of any apparitions for a few years. Popular tradition now holds that the ghosts reappear every four years – so by that reckoning the next sighting should take place on 29 March 2008 – I await with interest to see if they reappear!

Nearby is the site of old Hinton Ampner House (SU 596275) which was reputed to be exceedingly haunted during a period of at least twenty years up to 1793 when the building was demolished. The present house, built away from the haunted site, has had, unfortunately, no supernatural activity and now forms, with the famous gardens, one of the most popular of the National Trust properties.

The first haunting of the old building occurred in 1755, when one of the stable lads claimed to have seen his former master, Lord Stawell, dressed in dark clothing and stumbling over the moonlit cobbles towards his former house. The building itself remained largely unoccupied for the next ten years with only the occasional visit being made by other members of Stawell family. Hence, in 1765, it was let to William Ricketts and his wife, Mary. William had made his money in Jamaica and was often away on business, which left Mary, his children and the servants at Hinton Ampner.

From the very outset the family were besieged by strange noises, which they were unable to account for. There was the sound of doors slamming and of footsteps walking along the upper corridors. The servants, who had accompanied the Ricketts from London, were especially perturbed and petitioned Mrs Ricketts to have the locks on all the doors changed; this was accordingly done but the noises still continued.

The troubles within the house steadily increased. The apparition of Lord Stawell was sighted again, this time in the house and this time by the nurse of one of the sons of the Ricketts. She too had come from London and had known nothing of the experience reported by the stable hand – yet the two tales tally perfectly in the detail of what the deceased owner looked like and was wearing.

By June 1771, along with the other supernatural activity, new phenomena appeared. Often the sound of conversation would come to the ears of the occupants of the house. At first a raised female voice would be heard, which was then joined by two distinct male voices. This would be followed by a series of crashes and screams which slowly died away. Despite the conversation being so loud not a single word was discernable – a common trait in hauntings of this type. One foolish nurse, Hannah Streeter, once made it known generally that she would like to hear more of the ghostly conversation – something which she was later to regret – for she was subjected to a constant rendition of the episode every night from then on.

Ghostly activity was centred around the bed chambers and in particular the yellow bedchamber. It was in this room that Mrs Ricketts and her children used to see a darkly dressed woman whose dress rustled as she moved about. Sometimes the sound of the dress could be heard brushing past the door and this was invariably loud enough to waken the occupant. After the apparition had faded there would often be the sound of groaning and occasionally the swish of the dress would remain in the room. Mrs Ricketts, who was often the centre of these events, also heard the sound of unusual music and a low murmuring, similar to the whispering of wind in a forest, which enveloped the whole house even on the stillest of evenings.

It passes without saying that searches were made of the property for intruders or those creating an elaborate hoax. At one time Mrs Ricketts' brother visited and stayed awake every night with a friend to try and catch whatever was causing the incidents. They were duly rewarded for their trouble since they were able to add greatly to the list of experiences recorded at Hinton Ampner. As well as the slamming of doors and the rustling of the dark lady they were treated to the sound of a gun discharging near where they sat, which was followed by hideous groans as though someone was dying. This sound may be explained the testimony of an old carpenter who had been summoned to the house a good number of years earlier to lift some floorboards for Lord Stewkeley who had owned the house until his death at the beginning of the eighteenth century. Apparently he had hidden something secret under the floor in the dining room – a murder perhaps?

So perplexing were the myriad of noises and sights that a reward was publicly offered for anyone able to rid the house of its unwanted co-tenants. This started at a mere £50 (a purchasing value of about £4,500 today) before rising to £100 by the time they left the house – it was never claimed.

Eventually the sounds forced the Ricketts to move from Hinton Ampner in 1771. Lodging was given to them by the Bishop of Winchester in Wolvesey Palace (see Wolvesey) where they remained until they moved back to London. The house was then taken on by the Lawrence family who managed to stifle the local talk of ghosts by threatening the servants. However, it appears that they too soon had enough of the manifestations which plagued the property for they left abruptly in 1773. The house then remained empty for a further twenty years since there was no family willing to take on the lease. Regarded as being too haunted for further human (at least temporal human) occupation it was finally demolished in 1793.

For a superb, full report of the haunting of Hinton Ampner I suggest they you find a copy of Peter Underwood's *Hauntings* (Dent, 1977) which contains an incredibly detailed and definitive account of this place.

Chilbolton (SU 394402)

The little village of Chilbolton is one of those places of which you think that time has passed it by. There are plenty of pretty Hampshire cottages and the villagers are friendly, welcoming the opportunity to chat with somebody about 'their' ghost.

It was here, in the fourteenth century Wherwell Abbey, that the root of this story is based. The abbey itself was very active from its foundation in 986 to its dissolution in 1539. There is no trace of the building above ground, though excavations forty years ago revealed a large layer of demolition in the grounds of the building known as The Priory.

Katherine Faulkner had been placed under the care of the nuns of the abbey and had taken holy orders largely against her will. In 1393 she escaped one night and spent the next seven years enjoying the life to which she had not been accustomed. As time went by she began to feel pangs of guilt for her disobedience to the Benedictine order she had left and resolved to return to the abbey and atone for her transgressions. Expecting to be welcomed back and forgiven she was instead hauled before a company of senior members of the abbey, including the Abbess, who tried her for all her wrongdoings during the time she had spent away. Her punishment was to be walled up alive in the cellars of the establishment, where she died.

Successive buildings have come and gone on this site and Chilbolton Rectory is now said to be haunted by her ghost. She is seen at the windows looking out at the world rushing past or sometimes silently beckoning to those who glimpse her.

Like so many stories of this kind there are many who are able to retell it and a fair number of people who know a friend-of-a-friend who has seen the apparition, but I have been unable to track down any first hand evidence – yet!

Wherwell is also the place where a mythical monster met its end. It has been said that a Cockatrice lived in the priory for a great number of years. A Cockatrice is not the sort of creature you would want to meet on a dark night being half cockerel and half lizard and I doubt it would be too popular at a zoo. A modern parallel is the basilisk in the Harry Potter stories. Theoretically it is quite easy to cultivate ones own Cockatrice. One only has to find an egg laid by a rooster, which is incubated by a toad. I would advise caution in trying this experiment at home – the resultant creature usually eats anyone and anything which gets in its way. It also has the annoying habit of turning people into stone by either them looking at it or it looking at them. If you do manage to kill a Cockatrice beware, it can still perform the petrifaction trick after death.

The monster in question had taken up living under the priory where it devoured maidens of the village (as all good monsters do) and despite vast rewards being put forward for its dispatch, the gold remained unclaimed. A passing nobleman, by the name of Henry Green, was tempted to kill the creature since he had run up vast gambling debts which needed to be paid off quickly, or else!

Pictures of Cockatrice are a little hard to
come by – here we have an artist's impression!

Making his plan carefully he went to the blacksmiths and had made an enormous shield of polished steel under which he could hide until he got to the lair of the Cockatrice. He had fashioned at the same time a mighty spear which he proposed to ram home into the heart of the monster to kill it. When these articles were ready he staggered off to the priory to start the combat. Bowed down with the weight of the bright shield he crawled the last few yards and called out in what he considered his best maiden-like voice. The great Cockatrice stirred and started to move towards him. Henry, cowering under his shield, prepared himself for the first blow and waited for the right moment to use his spear. Suddenly there was a noise like a thousand claps of thunder and all became quiet. Henry, still cowering, was confused: where was the attack he had been expecting? Cautiously he raised the shield and to his horror saw that the Cockatrice was rearing above him – yet something was not quite right. It wasn't moving. Its scales had the look of limestone and its feathers appeared as though they were made of sandstone. He got up and thrust his spear into the beast which shattered into a thousand lumps of stone on the spot killing poor Henry. However, he had done his job and the village was freed from the tyranny of the monster. Unbeknown to Henry, the Cockatrice, sensing an assailant, tried to turn him to stone but had its glare cast back at itself in the mirrored shield and became itself petrified through its own petrifaction process!

Chilworth

Chilworth is situated to the west of Eastleigh and Walnut Cottage is the perfect haunted country cottage. The haunting of this building has been quite widely documented and it makes a very interesting study.

Until the mid-1980s it had been occupied by the same family for at least three generations – and during that time the seventeenth century cottage had been the site of many unexplainable happenings. During the middle of the nineteenth century the place had effectively been abandoned due to the ghostly presences felt, seen and heard here.

Much of what is known to have taken place here is due to the accounts Mrs MacRae, whose family lived in the house, submitted to the *Evening Echo* during 1972 which describe a fair number of the events encountered.

Possibly the most striking aspect about the case have been the instances where strange balls of light have been seen inside and attached to the house. Inside, they have been seen casting a light on the floor which can not be traced back to other, natural lights, such as the rays of the setting sun. Outside, the light was once seen attached to the stack of the chimney and casting a bright glow over the whole of the roof. This was in 1940 and the MacRaes, who noticed them as they were walking home, were convinced that their house was on fire and the glow was emanating from brightly burning roof timbers and thatch. Hurrying the last 100 yards they were astonished to find that not only had the light vanished from the cottage but there was no damage to the building whatsoever.

Similar accounts of great balls of light have been witnessed many times and in a whole assortment of locations. Scientifically they can often be explained as examples of ball lightning, a scantly understood phenomenon, which occurs naturally in the environment. These balls can last for several minutes according to eye-witnesses and have some interesting properties. While some burn everything they touch and destroy electrical wiring others take on the properties akin to a football – some have even been known to bounce down stairs leaving no damage behind. Recent work in the field has come up with some new theories to support the existence of this spectacle and current work has even managed to produce, to a degree, these balls. They are thought to be caused by the discharge of electricity during a lightning strike which leaves a molten hole within the atmosphere. This in turn absorbs and burns surrounding material which has been disturbed by the initial strike while maintaining a ball shape due to the gravitational pull it exerts.

While this theory goes some way to explain ball lightning (at least it acknowledges its existence) it does not explain the myriad of characteristics which have been witnessed. To this case we can apply the theory and hypothesise that after a lightning strike the dust on the roof could have been absorbed and ignited. Even in the case of Walnut Cottage it does not explain the lack of damage to the building or why it has occurred at least once inside the property. This remains something of a mystery.

The most frequent of the other hauntings which besiege the house appear to be the sound of footsteps in one place or another. A favourite place for footsteps to be heard is on the stairs, ascending and descending. This sound has been heard by at least three members of the MacRae family over a period of 100 years and at least once subsequently.

The cottage itself originally formed two tiny houses built for the estate on whose boundary it lies. It had been used for a while as a school and the MacRae's operated it as a guest house for a while. A report in 1922 from a Mr and Mrs Withers mentions the fact that they stay was not altogether peaceful. Awakened early one morning from a fitful sleep they were distressed to notice that their eiderdown was glowing strongly, although no heat was emitting from it. Others who stayed were also troubled: some left halfway though the night, refusing to stay a moment longer in such a haunted house!

A starting noise, soon to become accustomed to in the MacRae household, was that of smashing china and general loud crashes. The nocturnal sounds of the house also became much louder. Speaking as someone who lives in an ancient cottage I can testify that old beams have an unerring ability to suddenly creak when it is silent elsewhere and any number of other strange noises can be heard on a regular basis when one is lying awake at night wishing that one was asleep! However, the sounds at Walnut Cottage were not often of this variety: they were more like the sound of a manic interior designer rearranging the furniture! Nothing was ever moved nor could any explanation ever be found.

Hursley (SU 420264)

One of the medieval castles rebuilt by Henry du Blois, whom we have met before at Wolvesey Castle, Merdon Castle can date its existence to the Iron Age much in the same way as St Catherine's Hill can. There is very little to see here these days of the motte and bailey although the still substantial earthworks can be discerned. The castle, along with the rest of the grounds which form Hursley Park, is owned by IBM. It is the setting for perhaps the most bizarre legend I have come across to date!

I suspect that at one time there were any number of ghosts active on this site given its connections Stephen and Matilda, Richard, son of Oliver Cromwell, and various other nobles of repute over the centuries. Last November I received a statement from a car driver passing along the road to Lower Slackstead who had observed a ball of mist move from one side of the road to the other near to the ruins of the castle. We are concerned however in this instance with the well that lies within what was the centre of the Norman defensive work. A local story tells that this well (now filled in) contains a remarkable power. Regarded by many, including several who you would think would scorn such an idea, to be bottomless; it also has the ability to pluck waterfowl!

At this point I suspect you the reader will be thinking that I have been the recipient of a tall tale told in the King's Head, Hursley to shut me up and get me to leave. This may well be the case but it would not account for the same story being recounted to me by an old lady who was cutting her hedge just along the road from the pub!

If one were to catch and take a duck to the well and drop it down the shaft it would mysteriously appear by the church in the centre of the village plucked and practically oven ready within seconds! I was unable to ascertain as to whether the bird was alive or not at the time of its reappearance or whether this marvel worked on any other type of fowl…

Hursley is also the location for a rare Hampshire vampire. Information on this being is a little hazy and there is a fair amount of the Bram Stoker Victorian melodrama worked into the stories I have heard. Apparently there lived in the village an unfortunate man by the name of Wool who committed suicide in about 1600. He was buried in unconsecrated ground near the crossroads. Within a month the local farmer noticed that some of his cattle had marks on them, as though they had been cut, and that they were not producing the milk they used to. Then sheep started to go missing only to be rediscovered 'bled bone dry with not a single drop of their blood left in them'. Suspicion centred on the suicide who was quickly exhumed before being reburied with a stake through the heart.

To some who tell the story, the legend persists; the vampire is still active and preys on any unsuspecting person foolish to be out of doors on at night when the moon is full and with their neck exposed!

Marwell Hall

Nowadays this building is used almost solely for weddings and conferences and other such activities redundant country houses are put to. It is set within the grounds of the internationally renowned Marwell Zoo which specialises in the breeding of rare or near-extinct species.

During the reign of Henry VIII Marwell passed to the Seymour family from the Bishops of Winchester. Sir Henry Seymour was not a likable person, always ready for a quarrel and there is still a popular story that, after a disagreement on the new Protestantism, he murdered the priest in the church at Owslebury, about a mile away from Marwell Hall. The priest, being a strong character and not dying immediately, had enough time to quote Psalm 109 and to curse both the house and the family. Whether there is any truth in this story remains to be seen, yet the fortunes of the Seymour family were short lived. Even the marriage of Jane Seymour to Henry VIII lasted less than a year.

There is one story, said to have taken place at Marwell, but which is repeated in several of the Hampshire country houses, which tells the sad legend of the Mistletoe Bough.

It was the evening after a wedding and the revelry and dancing was at its height. The young bride, with a sprig of mistletoe pinned to her dress, tiring of the dance suggested that they play a game of hide and seek which was greeted with enthusiasm by all present. Off she dashed to find a suitable hiding place while the others waited the allotted time. The search began and as the hours and days passed her whereabouts remained a mystery. Finally they gave up the hunt with the conclusion reached that she had abandoned her husband on their wedding night. Several years later when a maid was hunting for some blankets she opened a large oak chest which had lain undisturbed in a quiet corner of the house. Inside were the skeletal remains of the bride with the sprig of mistletoe still pinned on her dress. She had hidden in the chest which was fitted with a lock which only opened from the outside… Her ghost is said to haunt the upstairs rooms of the building searching in vain for her husband, as he had searched in vain for her.

One previous housemaid of Marwell Hall left an account of a strange apparition which could be directly related to the above story. Apparently on 27 December if one was to stray away from your bedroom after 11.00 p.m. you would be confronted with a large group of youngsters seemingly dashing from room to room and from floor to floor. Could this be the vibrations left by a frantic search party looking for the young bride?

Returning to Tudor England we meet Henry VIII and Jane in the May of 1536. Legend tells us that they were married here in the Great Hall even before the axe had fallen on the unfortunate neck of Anne Boleyn. Jane produced an heir for Henry but died in that same childbirth less than a year after they had been married. From then on both the ghosts of Jane and Anne have been sighted around the building and an area known as the Yew Tree Walk. Probably most surprisingly it is Anne who has been the most frequent visitor, and by all accounts she is a lively ghost with at least seven other haunted palaces and houses claiming her ghost as their own. She is often seen preceding a calamity or the death of the owner of the house and is considered to be the vengeful wraith of Anne Boleyn bringing doom on the family which ultimately caused her fall from grace.

At Marwell there is also one of those little country sayings which usually appear to be unfounded and then confound us as they come true! At one time there was a path which led from the hall to the main road to Owslebury through a doorway let into the wall. It was frequently passed around the locals and staff of the hall that if the doorway should ever become blocked then the wall around the door would crumble and fall down. This cautionary tale was ignored one day and the doorway was bricked up. Within a few months the walls on either side were nothing more than piles of mouldering masonry!

Micheldever (SU 513391)

Micheldever is a quiet village with a spectacular country church. What the building lacks in size it makes up for in sheer originality. Inserted into the otherwise nondescript medieval nave is a great octagon completed in brick in 1808. This outlandish piece of architecture, which would have been considered novel almost two centuries later, gives the building a unique atmosphere. The chancel with its wonderful reredos of mosaic *opus sectile* (an under-recognised Victorian art form) is also to be recommended. Yet it is within the churchyard that we must look for our ghost and only then on a snowy day.

The agricultural riots which occurred in this area during 1830 and 1831 were the scene of some of the most brutal of clashes between law enforcers and manual workers. The punishments dispensed by the judicial system were typical of the time and noteworthy only for their harsh sentencing.

A local worker, a young man by the name of Henry Cook, was involved in one of the riots and during the course of the fight knocked off the hat of one Justice Bingham Baring. Taken before the assizes at Winchester he was tried for attempted murder. With the guilty verdict pronounced there was only one punishment suitable for the crime – hanging. Henry was executed for knocking off a hat.

His body was brought back to the village with great dignity; in his death he had become a martyr for the cause. He was buried in the churchyard under a simple slab near to the church.

His grave has long since been lost but the legend persists that no matter how hard it snows the grave of the martyr will always remain clear.

Twyford (SU 481246)

One of the more persistent tales told hereabouts relates to the ghost of a lone cyclist who is often seen passing along the lanes in Twyford and nearby Shawford. Seemingly dressed in the period of the early 1930s he gently pedals his slightly antiquated machine (although not out of keeping!) slowly along as though with no apparent purpose. Within the past year he has been spotted quite a few times by people conscious that they have seen a ghost, and probably many further times by those thinking that it is just another 'old boy' on his slow way home from his allotment.

In January 2006 alone the cyclist was reported to me by no fewer than four people; two even saw him on the same night! The first report on 12 January stated that, and I quote, 'this youngish chap in plus fours and cap slowly came along the road to Shawford over Norris' Bridge before disappearing.'

The second came on the afternoon of the fourteenth when it was noted that a cyclist suddenly appeared in the middle of the road in front of a car before dematerialising at the precise point where the car would have hit it! Suffice to say the driver was still very shocked when relating this tale to me a few days later.

Perhaps the most interesting observation is a dual sighting on 27 January. Another cyclist, commuting back to the village from Winchester, noticed the bobbing of a red rear cycle lamp in front of him while going along Church Lane (SU 481254). Since it was moving slowly the terrestrial cyclist increased speed to overtake. The outline of the bicycle itself came into view and the biker looked down to select a faster gear. On looking up the phantom had disappeared.

A short while later another cyclist following the same road reported being chased by a cyclist with the dull white glow of the front light of a bicycle slowly catching up with her. Looking back she saw the hazy outline of a figure on an older machine a few yards away from her. It appeared that the front light was bobbing about more than hers; as though the bicycle was riding on much rougher, perhaps unmade road surface. This pursuit continued until the lady cyclist reached the entrance to St Mary's church – and at that point the light vanished abruptly. The ghost was again spotted by a couple walking up Hazeley Road on 6 May 2006!

The Mildmay family played an important role in the development of Twyford and the surrounding area. It was they who gained possession of Marwell and Twyford manors after the Seymour family fell from royal favour (see Marwell Hall) and who did much in the way of rebuilding work to their various estates. One such reconstruction was undertaken by Henry Mildmay in the 1660s to Twyford Manor utilising material salvaged from the ecclesiastical part of Marwell. The building retains an air of medieval grandeur and is known now as 'The

The spot in Church Lane Twyford where the ghostly cyclist was seen twice one day in January 2006.

Monastery.' There are indications that the cellars of this building were used to house errant monks while they undertook their penance – and not all of them seem to have left. One such monk is supposed to roam through the rooms of the building while another has been seen from time to time walking from 'The Monastery' towards Brewers Lane over the forecourt of Ivan Stacey's garage (SU 480243).

Another spectral dog is seen on the water meadows known as Twyford Meads (SU 476 254) fairly infrequently. This is just as well since the hound has the unfriendly characteristics of a 'Shuck' and one would do well never to meet it!

Black Shuck, as the generic spectre is known, is traditionally associated with East Anglia and folklore on the Norfolk and Suffolk coast. However, reports of a giant dog have been reported all over the country and during different eras. They have been written about in song and story – Conan Doyle's *Hound of The Baskervilles* being a classic example – and have a variety of attributes, mainly unlucky or evil. Several other ghost dogs are reported in Hampshire (see the case in the Water Meadows in Winchester), but the Shuck is something completely different; it is usually described as a direct incarnation of the devil.

This particular example is described as being the size of a small cow – many are portrayed as being calf-like – and has great blazing eyes! The last report I have heard concerns a farm labourer on his way home, towards the end of the eighteenth century. He had finished his work

Norris' Bridge Twyford, where the phantom cyclist was hit by a passing car!

for the day and was walking along the towpath of the Itchen navigation that runs through this area. As he took the path from the canal to the church he suddenly noticed a great bounding dog running unswervingly towards him from the direction of the village. Its coat was black and glossy as fresh tar and its eyes glowed with a fire 'directly from the pit of hell!' The farm worker immediately turned on his track and jumped into the river where he hid until the monster had passed him by…

On recounting this story to some friends of mine it was pointed out that this is just the sort of tale we would tell if we had been to the pub too long, had had too much to drink and had fallen in the river on our way home – how else would you explain the reason for being so wet to your wife than to say you were chased by a Shuck?

Within the very heart of this 'Queen of Hampshire Villages' there lies the quiet Queen Street. Along this road there are reputed to be at least three haunted houses. One, which occupies the corner halfway along the road, is said to be haunted by the infrequent return of a lady who was murdered there. Occasionally the apparition is seen but more often the occupants were made aware of her presence by the smell of the ubiquitous 'Lilly-of-the-valley'. Residents of another house, almost opposite, used to report the sound of a movement in an upstairs room. So perturbed were the occupants when they first heard the noises that they had the house exorcised. Now they appear to be quite remorseful over having banished their ghosts.

The third haunting is something of an oddity. On the night of Sunday 31 July 2005 the occupants went to bed as usual. On awakening the following morning they were exceedingly disconcerted to find that six of the nine clocks in the house had stopped around midnight.

Four of these clocks were battery operated while the other two were clockwork driven. Of the latter, one dated from the 1920s and was very reliable, while the other was a cheap mantle clock from the 1960s. Those powered by batteries varied in age from less than one year to about seven years old.

No logical explanation can be found for this stoppage of timepieces, especially as several remained unaffected. Whether this was the date of a previous death in the house, during an era when the clocks were stopped to mark the passing, or something to do with the ancient festival of Lughnasadh, we can only hypothesize. The occupants of the house had reported nothing untoward before that event although they await with interest the morning of 1 August 2006!

As a final footnote to Twyford and some other of the villages hereabouts; beware of hitch-hikers. It seems that a number of years ago a young lady was killed on the road to Colden Common and since then has a habit of flagging down passing cars and asking for a lift to the next village. The first the inkling the unwary driver has of the ghostly nature of his passenger is when she suddenly disappears!

Upham

Lying to the east of Eastleigh and to the north of Bishops Waltham lies the delightful hamlet of Upham. This village, whose poor house had a rule that all should attend church on Sunday on pain of forfeiting their dinner, is now very much part of the affluent area of rural Hampshire. Cromwell once stayed in the Brushmakers Arms and stabled his horses in the church. It remains on record that it cost the parishioners the sum of 2s 6d to have the church cleaned in time for Christmas due to the mess the horses had made.

Strangely the area was the conurbation for those who practiced the trade of brush making and our first haunting recounts the tale of one unfortunate fellow.

Mr Chicket was a miser – of that there was no doubt. He made and sold brushes of a high quality but refused to spend even the smallest amount of money on anything. Being an untrusting fellow he kept all his money on himself and slept with it in a bag under his pillow. One night as he was sleeping in a cheap room in the Brushmakers Arms his room was entered and he was murdered for his wealth. It was not long before gossip started to circulate within the community stating that the ghost of Mr Chicket had been seen returning to the place where he had died to seek revenge, for the perpetrators of the crime had not been caught.

During recent times the dog of one of the landlords of the pub has refused to enter the room in question. It has sat resolutely in the doorway, hackles up and growling at some unseen entity. While the tale is looked upon by those drinking in the pub as being laughable I was unable to find anyone who would spend any time in the room on their own.

Within the village there is also a house which appears to be haunted by a strange, but rather beautiful smell. It appears that a strong perfume is randomly smelt at different times and in different places around the house. It comes and goes in a matter of moments but has perplexed the owners who are convinced it is nothing to do with their imagination. One day a neighbour commented on the smell, enquiring as to what new brand of washing power the owner was using! This haunting is probably one of the most delightful I have come across and makes a pleasant change from foreboding atmospheres and spectral monks!

five

THE LEGEND OF SLEEPERS HILL

It was the famous wordsmith Malory who first wrote openly stating that Winchester was, and should be recognised as, the ancient Arthurian seat of Camelot. However for years before, and after, the city had been held in very high esteem by those researching the once and future king. During the reign of Henry VII the interest reached its peak. The round table that continues to be hung in the Great Hall was repainted as a mark of respect; for it was believed then to be the round table at which Arthur and his knights sat. The King's belief in Winchester being Camelot was such that when his wife Elizabeth was pregnant he sent her down to give birth to her first son here and to name him Arthur – destining him to be a great king.

Unfortunately, Arthur never became king, dying before his father, who left the crown to his second son, the notorious Henry VIII. One wonders what the country would have been like had not Arthur Tudor died.

This is one of several stories told about a small wooded slope that can be found just outside Winchester. To this day the hill, although extensively built upon with expensive luxury houses, retains an air of mystery and foreboding which even the brightest sunlight can not dispel. Imagine then what it would have been like when the city was still very small and the whole area teemed with legend.

The legend centres on a solid figure in history, His Grace, Peter de la Roche who was for some time Bishop of Winchester and was the Archbishop who crowned Henry III king in 1216 and the account of what happened to him was recorded in the fourteenth-century *Chronicon de Lanercost*. The story detailed below has only a passing similarity to the original, having been embellished and extended over the centuries.

The event is said to have happened one bright and fair day when he was hunting in the forest just outside of the city walls. He became detached from the rest of the hunt and became lost to them. Wandering back northwards towards Winchester he came across a knight in full armour who led him to a glade on the side of the slope. On entering the clearing the Bishop found it to be empty, but as he waited, as the knight had told him, a fair and beautiful maiden appeared from out of the hillside. The maiden passed across to the Bishop and bade him to follow her into the hill as he had been invited to dine with the king! This was an invitation that could not be refused and Peter duly followed her.

Once inside he was shown a table that had been set for a great feast and as soon as he had been seated, in marched this group of knights headed by a great chieftain. This King sat and the Bishop found himself placed at the right hand of the monarch. At this point he could stand the suspense no longer and fearing that he was about to be taken as hostage by some uprising asked the king who he was. The monarch replied that he was indeed King Arthur; the once and future king of these lands. As the meal wore on so conversation became easier and it transpired that one day in every seven years Arthur was allowed to awaken from his enchanted sleep and eat with his pure knights. However, time had also worn on and the Bishop had been expected back from hunting many hours previously and he felt he could not return with such a tale without some proof of what had happened. He challenged Arthur on this point, who agreed. The king ordered Peter to close his right hand and Peter did so. Then the king commanded him to open it again and as the Bishop's hand opened out flew a butterfly. From that day on he became famous for his power over butterflies and he was able to produce on demand, even in the Cathedral, even in winter a butterfly as testament to his story. And from that day on Peter became known as the Bishop of the Butterflies and the slope gained the name of Sleepers Hill after those who rest under it who will return when the country is in dire need.

Other local titles published by Tempus

Haunted Cornwall
PAUL NEWMAN

For anyone who would like to know why Cornwall is called the most haunted place in Britain, this collection of stories of apparition, manifestations and related supernatural incidents from around the Duchy provides the answer. From heart-stopping accounts of poltergeists to first-hand encounters with ghouls and spirits who haunt prehistoric graves, *Haunted Cornwall* contains a chilling range of ghostly phenomena.

0 7524 3668 6

Haunted Kent
JANET CAMERON

Haunted Kent contains chilling tales from around the county, including the hunchbacked monk at Boughton Malherbe, the black dog of Leeds and the well-known tale of Lady Blanche of Rochester Castle. This fascinating collection of strange sightings and happenings in the county's streets, churches, public houses and country lanes is sure to appeal to anyone wanting to know more about the ghostly history of Kent.

0 7524 3605 8

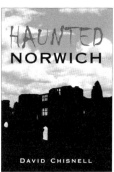

Haunted Norwich
DAVID CHISNELL

Haunted Norwich contains spooky stories from around the city, including the old witch who wanders up and down Bishopsgate, the Lady in Grey who was locked up alive in her house during the plague of 1578 and others who are said to haunt the city's infamous Tombland area. This collection of strange happenings in the city is sure to appeal to anyone wanting to know more about the haunted heritage of Norwich.

0 7524 3700 3

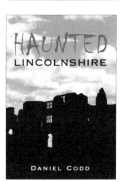

Haunted Lincolnshire
DANIEL CODD

Drawing on historical and contemporary sources, Haunted Lincolnshire contains a chilling range of ghostly phenomena. From tales of spectral monks at Lincoln's medieval cathedral and the highwayman who wanders the old coach yard of the fourteenth-century White Hart Hotel, to stories of the Green Lady at Thorpe Hall and sightings of the demon dog known as Black Shuck, this phenomenal gathering of ghostly goings-on is bound to captivate anyone interested in the supernatural history of the area.

0 7524 3817 4

If you are interested in purchasing other books published by Tempus, or in case you have difficulty finding any Tempus books in your local bookshop, you can also place orders directly through our website

www.tempus-publishing.com